Mind, Religion and Health, With an Appreciation of the Emmanuel Movement; How Its Principles Can Be Applied in Promoting Health and in the Enriching of Our Daily Life

MIND, RELIGION
AND HEALTH

WITH AN APPRECIATION OF
THE EMMANUEL MOVEMENT

*How Its Principles Can Be Applied in Promoting Health
ana in the Enriching of our Daily Life*

BY

ROBERT MacDONALD

Minister of the Washington Avenue Church, Brooklyn, New York

FUNK & WAGNALLS COMPANY
NEW YORK AND LONDON
1908

CONTENTS

[iii]

CONTENTS

[v]

CONTENTS

[vi]

CONTENTS

INTRODUCTION

SCIENTIFIC AND RELIGIOUS
CONDITIONS

We have seen the spring sun shine out of an empty heaven to light up a soulless earth. We have felt with utter loneliness that the Great Companion is dead. Our children, it may be hoped, will know that sorrow only by the reflex light of a wondering compassion.—PROFESSOR CLIFFORD.

> *I can believe this dread machinery*
> *Of sin and sorrow would confound me, else*
> *Devised—all pain, at most expenditure*
> *Of pain by who devised, pain to evolve*
> *By new machinery in counterpart*
> *The moral qualities of man—how else?—*
> *To make him love in turn and be beloved;*
> *Creative end, self-sacrificing too,*
> *And thus eventually godlike.*
>
> —BROWNING.

> *Speak to Him, thou, for He hears, and*
> *Spirit with spirit can meet;*
> *Closer is He than breathing*
> *And nearer than hands and feet.*
>
> —TENNYSON.

INTRODUCTION

SCIENTIFIC AND RELIGIOUS CON-DITIONS

As sanction for publishing a volume on mental and religious therapeutics, it may not be amiss to glance at the scientific and religious conditions that call for such consideration, or at least endue it with profound interest. While it is an eminently questioning age, more so than any preceding age in the world's history, the tendency of investigation is undoubtedly spiritual. The former material hypothesis as to the origin of life, its constituent elements, its order of manifestation, its manifold phenomena can not claim the most trustworthy scientific and philosophic authority. While we are still in the grip of biological and evolutionary principles—a grip that gives no promise of weakening—with their varied protoplasms, atoms, and life-germs, matter as the universal cosmic reality with mind, its product, claims not even serious scientific attention. The protoplasm from which the higher forms of life has been evolved is seen to be that into which life was involved by creative energy existing quite distinct therefrom. The doctrine of biogenesis—life from a living germ—is the concession of as scientifically consistent biologists as Huxley, Darwin, and Spencer. And tho these are content to leave unnamed the origin of that life, leaving perforce that far-away beginning clothed in mystery, nevertheless Wallace, who made commendable spiritistic strides in later life, Le Conte in his "Evolution and Its Relation to Religious Thought," Henry Drummond in his "Ascent of Man," and Sir Oliver Lodge hesitate not to introduce a divine life power into their biological origins, thus moralizing the evolutionary philosophy and immeasurably universalizing its scope.

In Haeckel's "Riddle of the Universe" we have an exposition of material evolution in its crassest form. The fundamental cosmic law that accounts for everything is the chemical law, the conservation of matter combined with the physical law, the conservation of energy. These, matter and energy, fill all space, occupy all time, and are the attributes of the substance of which the universe is made. All living protoplasm springs from what he calls the chemical and physical properties of carbon, which confer a peculiar power on its albuminoid compounds. Notice the conclusions from this atheistic hypothesis. This cellular theory, Haeckel affirms, has given us the first true interpretation of the physical, chemical, and even psychological processes of life.[1] Further, that consciousness and thought are functions of the ganglionic cells of the cortex of the brain. Further still, that attraction and repulsion are the sources of the human and animal will.[2] And finally that the soul is the operation of a group of cells.[3] Haeckel hesitates not to say that freedom of will is an illusion, that man's existence clearly begins and ends with his temporal body, and that God and the world are one, the idea of God being identical with that of nature or substance.[4] It was of Haeckel's pantheism that Schopenhauer said, "Pantheism is only a polite form of atheism, for it means the destruction of the dualistic

[1] Haeckel's "Riddle of the Universe," p. 103.
[2] *Ibid.*, p. 45.   [3] *Ibid.*, p. 77.   [4] *Ibid.*, p. 122.

antithesis of God and the world in its recognition that the world exists in virtue of its own inherent force."[1] Sir Oliver Lodge says in his "Life and Matter": "Haeckel thought he was interpreting Darwin. But Darwin never sanctioned his conclusion that everything is blind chance without aim or special purpose."[2] Lodge further affirms "that Huxley repudiated materialism as a satisfactory and complete scheme of things and disagreed with Haeckel's position.[3] Berkeley's answer to the materialistic theory of creation is worthy of note, "If the materialist affirms that the universe and all its phenomena are resolvable into matter and motion, what you call matter and motion are known to us only as forms of consciousness, and the existence of a state of consciousness apart from a thinking mind is a contradiction in terms."[4]

To show the fallacies of Haeckel's materialistic science four treatises were written, each exerting far-reaching theistic and Christian influence: Lodge's "Life and Matter,"

[1] Schopenhauer's "The World as Will and Idea," p. 103.
[2] Sir Oliver Lodge, "Life and Matter," p. 97.
[3] *Ibid.*, p. 282.   [4] *Ibid.*, p. 239.

Kidd's "Social Evolution," Drummond's "Ascent of Man," and Balfour's "Foundations of Belief." Of these the first mentioned is the most critical, the last three the most constructive and of popular intent. Lodge, with true scientific insight, shows the fallacy in each of Haeckel's propositions, and concludes: "We know that a complex piece of matter called the brain is the instrument of mind and consciousness. When stimulated, mental activity results; when injured or destroyed, no manifestation of mental activity is possible. Brain is the means by which mind is made manifest on this material plane, but mind is not limited to its material manifestation, nor can we maintain that without matter mind, intellect, consciousness have no sort of existence. It is through the region of ideas and intention of mind that we become aware of the existence of matter. The soul of a thing is its underlying permanent reality, that which gives it its meaning and confers upon it its attributes. The body is a mechanism for the manifestation of what else would be imperceptible." [1]

[1] Lodge, "Life and Matter," p. 108.

[7]

Altho Kidd's "Social Evolution" is by no means a strong and satisfactory refutation of materialism, being full of glaring inconsistencies, it is a brave and laborious attempt for emancipation from the evolutionary grip. Kidd's weakness is seen in such questionable, if not erroneous, propositions as these: "Man's reason is inimical to progress." "Social science is on an ultrarational basis."[1] "Man must become irrational to progress."

It was because of such premises that Professor Sidgwick said, "Kidd left social science where he found it." Another critic condemned the work as the most ignorant book of modern times. It should be recalled, however, that Sidgwick was a hedonist; and that his unnamed critic was a materialistic evolutionist.

Balfour's "Foundations of Belief" attacks the evolutionary hypothesis upon its naturalistic assumption that the materialistic theory of creation is the only one that can possibly account for the origin of the universe, and that at no point in the line of development

[1] Kidd's "Social Evolution," p. 42.

from atom to atom can a non-material agency be put in. Balfour's Christian convictions can not tolerate such atheism. What he calls "the circuit of belief" must have more spirit-istic foundation than a naturalistis basis. "Naturalism," he exclaims, "is the result of the rationalizing methods applied with pitiless consistency to the whole circuit of belief." [1] It is needless to say he places the foundations of belief in Revelation, theological and ontological arguments, the religious instincts, the soul's longing for God, and in what he calls the reality of experience. "Compare," he says, "the central truth of theology, there is a God, with one of the fundamental presuppositions of science, there is an independent material world. . . While it has been found by many not only possible but easy to doubt the existence of God, doubts as to the independent existence of matter have assuredly been confined to the rarest moments of subjective reflection, and have dissolved at the first touch of what we are pleased to call reality."

[1] Balfour's "Foundations of Belief," p. 172.
[2] *Ibid.*, p. 235.

In Drummond's "Ascent of Man" we find a tactful acceptance of evolution, but stript of its naturalistic beginnings. He sees it to be a divinely chosen method, full of moral purpose, and run through and through with altruistic motive and under the divine superintendence at every stage of development. His comforting word is: "As there was clearly a moral purpose in the end to be achieved by evolution, should we not expect to find some similar purpose in the means? Can we perceive no high design in selecting this particular method, no worthy ethical result which should justify the conception as well as the execution of evolution?"[1] Drummond's evolutionary altruism is exprest in such a passage as this: "Love is not a late arrival, an afterthought with creation. Its roots began to grow with the first cell of life which budded in the earth."[2] It should be observed that more scientific and less religious minds than Drummond's sanction this altruistic conviction. Spencer states that "the most general conclusion is that in the order of obligation

[1] Drummond, "Ascent of Man," p. 93.
[2] *Ibid.*, p. 276.

the preservation of the species takes precedence over the preservation of the individual where the two conflict."[1] And Huxley states that "the practise of that which is ethically best—what we call goodness—involves a course of conduct which in all respects is opposed to that which leads to success in the cosmic struggle for existence."[2] One of Drummond's most theistic sentences is this, "What is that in which things live and move and have their being? It is nature, the cosmos, and something more—some one more, an Infinite Intelligence, and an Eternal Will. Everything that lives lives in virtue of its correspondence with this environment. Evolution is not to unfold from within, but to infold from without."[3] Drummond would not admit that the lower includes the higher, that the mind and moral nature come from the atom. To the contrary, he asserts it has been a great mistake to interpret nature from the standpoint of the atom. Instead of abolishing a creative hand, he claims, evolution

[1] Spencer, "Principles of Ethics," pt. 2, p. 6.
[2] Huxley, "Evolution and Ethics," p. 33.
[3] Drummond, p. 412.

[11]

demands it. While Spencer exclaims that matter in its ultimate nature is as incomprehensible as space or time, Drummond exclaims: "This is a spiritual not a material universe. Evolution is advolution, the phenomenal expression of the Divine, the progressive realization of the ideal."[1] While Huxley wavers between biogenesis and abiogenesis—living matter from non-living—affirming without hesitation the former position, but not daring to deny the possibility of the latter; and while Spencer defines life "as the continuous adjustment of internal relations to external relations,"[2] making much of the correspondence between certain inner physicochemical actions, and certain outer physicochemical actions, Le Conte boldly affirms that evolution is one thing and materialism quite another, and again that no more should evolution negative our belief in God as creator of the universe than should gravitation or any other law of nature."[3]

All this is what is meant in saying the scientific tendency is spiritualistic. The

[1] Drummond, p. 340. [2] Spencer, "First Principles," p. 70.
[3] Le Conte, "Evolution and Religious Thought," p. 277.

matter, and that an orderly, designful divine thought runs through everything.

A still further scientific principle is ours to share, and quite basal to the position taken in this volume. It is what is known as the molecular theory of existence.[1] Not only within and beyond the protoplasmic cell is there divine life energy; not only is evolution mysteriously related to an infinite and spiritual involution, with a spiritual germ primary, and the material germ secondary, and the phenomenal product thereof; but everything, even the hardest, most compact solids are composed of tiny moving particles in a constant state of rapid vibration, and as distinct from one another as are the individual material forms of which these are composed. The flintiest granite, the hardest, most compact, steel is thus constituted, as well as the most limpid liquids, the most ethereal gases and the most attenuated ether. No existing solid mass, nor thinnest fluid, but that finer substances and forces could be inserted between

---

[1] For a full and very technical discussion of this theory see Lord Kelvin's "Molecular Dynamics and Wave Theory of Light."

demands it. While Spencer exclaims that matter in its ultimate nature is as incomprehensible as space or time, Drummond exclaims: "This is a spiritual not a material universe. Evolution is advolution, the phenomenal expression of the Divine, the progressive realization of the ideal."[1] While Huxley wavers between biogenesis and abiogenesis—living matter from non-living—affirming without hesitation the former position, but not daring to deny the possibility of the latter; and while Spencer defines life "as the continuous adjustment of internal relations to external relations,"[2] making much of the correspondence between certain inner physicochemical actions, and certain outer physicochemical actions, Le Conte boldly affirms that evolution is one thing and materialism quite another, and again that no more should evolution negative our belief in God as creator of the universe than should gravitation or any other law of nature."[3]

All this is what is meant in saying the scientific tendency is spiritualistic. The

[1] Drummond, p. 340.   [2] Spencer, "First Principles," p. 70.
[3] Le Conte, "Evolution and Religious Thought," p. 277.

latest conviction of science is that the creation of the world is through an evolutionary process, but if a process, then from a divine beginning, but further, a process that reveals the immanence of this Divine Creator at every stage. We conservative religionists can no longer ignore the evolutionary principle upon the excuse that it compromises us to materialism on the one side and a lowdown type of animalistic ancestry on the other. Evolution is both theistic in its inception and universal in its application, not only illustrating but proving the existence of God at every step. Everything that exists throughout nature's wide domain has been a slow, patient, continuous development, but from something that previously existed in the mind of God. Everything to the smallest atom of matter contains and expresses divine design. Each cause is the effect of some cause a little more remote. Thus does each discovered fact bind us definitely, designfully, relentlessly into that infinite series of causes and effects that accounts for this divinely ordered cosmic existence.

This orderly creative process is continuing

to-day as truly as in any most distant century
of time. The miraculous is thus eliminated
from creation and our consciousness thereof,
because God has ever been immanent in the
one, and has lately taken up permanent residence in the other. Everything from dull
atom to shining star, including the mind and
body of man, is law-formed organism pulsing
with energy and athrill with life, receiving
meaning from its relation to the God-super-
intended whole.

> All are but parts of one stupendous whole
> Whose body nature is and God the soul.

And as the clear-seeing Wordsworth exclaims,

> In the round ocean, and the living air,
> And the blue sky, and in the Mind of Man

Verily, the poets at a single intuitive bound
reach the heights up which the scientists
climb with ponderous and cautious step. But
favored indeed are both religionists and poet
to possess scientific affirmation that law
reigns supreme, reducing all fragmentary
events and varying modes of motion into sub-
limest system; that there is no dead and inert

[14]

matter, and that an orderly, designful divine thought runs through everything.

A still further scientific principle is ours to share, and quite basal to the position taken in this volume. It is what is known as the molecular theory of existence.[1] Not only within and beyond the protoplasmic cell is there divine life energy; not only is evolution mysteriously related to an infinite and spiritual involution, with a spiritual germ primary, and the material germ secondary, and the phenomenal product thereof; but everything, even the hardest, most compact solids are composed of tiny moving particles in a constant state of rapid vibration, and as distinct from one another as are the individual material forms of which these are composed. The flintiest granite, the hardest, most compact, steel is thus constituted, as well as the most limpid liquids, the most ethereal gases and the most attenuated ether. No existing solid mass, nor thinnest fluid, but that finer substances and forces could be inserted between

[1] For a full and very technical discussion of this theory see Lord Kelvin's "Molecular Dynamics and Wave Theory of Light."

the molecules. These constituent particles are ever susceptible to the expansions of heat and the contractions of cold. No material form is stable. No solid mass can resist chemical action is the statement of the scientist. Speaking theistically, we say no solid can withstand the subtle invisible manifestations of that force infinite that expresses itself in the particles of matter which at one time dissolves them into rapid vibration, at another forces them to appear and disappear in ever-varying combinations.

All this applies to the human frame. In our flesh tissue, muscles, and nerves it is a constant process of contraction and expansion. Every mental state, every emotional condition, has its contracting and expanding work to do throughout the physical organs, the minute cells, and the more minute aggregation of microscopic molecules. They all can be drawn at will closer together or forced wider apart without in the least disturbing the unity of the body. Disease makes for contraction, density, inertness. Health radiates its warmth throughout the fleshy mass, inducing motion, separation of the molecules, and circulation of the life energy, as does the sun's heat break up the solid ice, liberating the liquid and gaseous particles therein.

The brain is as susceptible to these chemical changes and more so than the body. The colder and more rigorous our thinking the greater the number of brain-cells that become inoperative, and the less circulatory the gray matter through them. The more emotional our mental processes become, the freer the brain action, and the larger become the number of brain-cells that respond to this warming, compelling force. Logical and scientific precision always sacrifices in breadth what it gains in intensity. Spiritual fervor induces mental comprehensiveness to the sacrifice of accuracy. Thus Darwin's lament over his loss of appreciation for music, general literature, and the entire esthetic side of a cultured life. But the privilege has been given to the entire scholastic world to praise him for that restriction of mental endeavor that enabled him to think out his splendid evolutionary hypothesis. Thus also we become intellectual mechanisms or men of broad culture as we throw our endeavor on the side of specialization, content to enlighten the world profoundly along a single line of some much-needed usefulness, else exert a broader, more esthetic, tho less strong and deep influence, and by way of recompense enjoying more, if achieving less of specific worth. The ideal life struggle before us all, and one that time is all too short to enable us to realize, is consistently to divide our efforts between the cold, calculating severe exercise that gives point and edge to our mental faculty and the warming, emotionalizing, spiritualizing of our mental equipment that vitalizes, broadens, and enlarges the greatest possible number of the many millions of brain-cells through which the divine life energy may circulate, radiating culture and the beneficent thrill of health throughout all the body's cells.

Much more needs to be declared than has yet been said or written upon the influences of our mental and emotional states upon the body's disease and health. The contracting and hardening, disease-enduring effects of hatred, anger, envy, doubt, and fear are not easily computed. Nor are the expanding liber-

Father is involved in the consideration with His sons and daughters living in time and space.

The scientific medium of this consideration will be psychology. It is already occupying the field with the world's eyes riveted upon its investigations and findings. Its companion in the research and discovery will be Christianity. They are by nature related, as both have to do with the psychic side of life. Revelation will furnish the rich content to the psychologic form. Psychology uncovers the potential depths of being in the human sphere. Christianity imparts to those depths infinite meaning. Psychology reveals the mental forces that shall be instrumental in the reconstruction of the life personal. Christianity shows those forces to be of divine origin. Psychology discovers a limitless subconscious human capacity, Christianity draws the curtain further still and reveals that realm of the individual limitless to be the finite manifestation of the universal life that is creative and remedial unto all the universe, including man. Psychology, because interested in all psychic conditions, asks for evidence of personal immortality the other side of death. Christianity has for two thousand years and more had acquaintance with the unseen world and waits to lay its evidence before every inquiring mind, and bring its assurances of the divine friendliness to every lonely troubled heart.

Henry Drummond not only spoke of religion and evolution being different sides of the same cosmic reality, but goes so far as to say that no reconciliation between evolution and Christianity is needed, because already one. "What is evolution?" he asks. "A method of creation. What is its object? To make more perfect living beings. What is Christianity? A method of creation. What is its object? To make more perfect human beings. Through what does evolution work? Through love. Through what does Christianity work? Through love. Evolution and Christianity have the same author, the same end, the same spirit." [1]

This intimated unity between psychology and Christianity needs the scientist and seer to show his dependent fellows that they are

[1] Drummond, "Ascent of Man," pp. 437, 438.

the two sides of the same psychic reality. James, Hudson, Myers, and a number of less well-known investigators have done the world inestimable service in disclosing the subconscious and subliminal realms. Wood and Dresser, through their fresh, strong inspirational thinking, are doing valiant pioneering upon both the spiritual and human sides of the heretofore great divide, and are elucidating deep things in their new thinking, clothed in simple and beautiful phraseology. Dubois, Sidis, Prince, Schofield and a hundred more along technical lines are turning psychologic knowledge unto therapeutic account, and are calling upon the entire medical profession to see and be convinced of the power of mind to cure many supposed bodily ills, in every case wherein the man is ill. The disciples of Christian Science and Faith Cure have wallowed in the dark to find the light, and found it, and without knowledge of psychology in the one, or scientific wielding of religious truth in the other have used certain psychologic and religious principles and made glad the heart of man. Only now is the Church awakening to the remedial power within its reach. Under what has become known as the Emmanuel movement the remedial work goes on. It is, so far, a distinctively practical movement for the curing of our ills. Here for the first time psychology and Christianity openly join hands and demonstrate each day their willingness to work together in a God-intentioned unity. For the first time physician and priest combine in psychotherapeutics against the ravages of disease. And in the cures wrought Dr. Worcester has already had multitudinous reward for his highly prized endeavor.

What the future holds along this line who can say? Whether the coming years will honor this last-mentioned form of the combined psychological and Christian method of restoring health only time can determine. All present-day theories and practises in the psychic treatment of disease are as yet pioneering attempts to unite in helpful working harmony the revelations of psychology and Christianity concerning the actual and potential natures of man, and of God; also the universe, to which both are related. But of this much we can be confident, that so beneficially divine a principle as that embodied in these different health movements will remain with the children of men. The vision beautiful will not depart. The principle once discovered can not be lost. God's near-by helpfulness that can be drawn on at will to satisfy the need, man's demonstrated ability to live henceforth a spiritually enriched and complete life, and the universe all athrill with recuperative life blessing for multitudinous sin-curst, disease-infected, world-tempted mortals, are truths that will abide.

This hopeful scientific condition of a more spiritual conviction concerning the origin and superintendence of the universe is also noticeable religiously. The present spiritual tendency of the Church can, however, be better stated in negative than positive terms. Its relinquishment of what is not conducive to the life of the spirit is more apparent than its achievements in that life. Its former dogmatism, for instance, has passed away never to return. While the Christian religion will always generate a theological side, and the age may be regarded as theological as any that has preceded, its theology is of a forma-

tive rather than of a dogmatic kind, more
questioning than confident of its doctrinal
positions. It is by no means to be deplored
that such grand old theologians as Calvin,
Jonathan Edwards, and Hodge have left
no successors. The scientific spirit of the age
precludes that, on the one side, and the quest
for truth, on the other. The cry of alarm over
the new theology is subsiding in view of our
growing consciousness of its need, and the
ever-present question of which new theology
is to be the most regretted, else the most welcomed as best expressive of an intelligent and
reasonable interpretation of the content of
the New Testament Scriptures. This search
for truth, that has been stimulated by the new
scholarship regardless of orthodox respecta-
bility and conformity to traditional standards, can not be too highly esteemed, as making for a profound intellectual openness, a
wide-reaching religious tolerance, and, best
of all, a larger, more devout Christian consciousness into which clearer visions of spiritual efficiency can come.

What, it may be asked, is the truth men
are seeking, men within and without the

Church, seeking along both scientific and religious lines? In the careful statement of Dr. George Gordon in his recent Edinburgh sermon (a sermon would that we all could feel the uplift of), it is in its supremest sense moral beings in relation one with another and with God. His definite word is: "The world of living souls with God in it is the truth. While it lives and while God lives in it we have the truth. Nothing that leaves God in the world, nothing that leaves men with souls in relations of obligation to one another and to God can dismay us. Behind all research, all science, all philosophy, all records, sacred or otherwise, we confess as the firm "set constitution of our world God and the sons of God in time."

This being truth, this being what Jesus came to reveal, this being what the Holy Spirit was sent to help us search for and find, it becomes a foregone conclusion that the complete finding of the truth is a very extensive undertaking; also that no one age of human thought and experience, conserved in creed and ecclesiastical organization, can adequately and satisfactorily formulate its

[27]

findings for a subsequent age. Just here the Church has not been always wise. It has insisted too often on uniformity of belief in behalf of that part of truth it found valuable, and which, to conserve and also make easy of acceptance, it has cut and dried, and done up into small, easily carried parcels, and labeled this and that. But it made two mistakes, one regarding the truth it would conserve; the other concerning the mind of man that was to receive it. It treated truth as tho it were a divine word that needed to be solemnized by councils and crystallized into dogma to make it authoritative, not knowing that the more it was authorized the more also it was devitalized. On the other hand, the Church should have seen truth to be a vital relationship with God, through which His remedial life flows, and out of which moral obligation springs.

Then how did it regard man's mind? Aggressive enough, and trustworthy thinking faculty on all possible matters, save religion, but there quite naïve and unreliable. The sad result has been that the Church has lost control of multitudes of the brightest minds in every age of its later history. The trouble is that the Church has not kept up with the age in which it has been placed. It would neither allow itself to become influenced by its fearless truth-seeking spirit, nor would it respect independent research lest its sacred tenets, however incomplete, its theological formulas, however mechanical, be disturbed and shown the need of revision. Thus it has always felt its mission to be to disregard the age, except to antagonize it. True it would save the age, but not at the price of concession unto its science, its culture, its truth. On the other hand, the age felt itself excusable for non-compliance with the terms of so narrow and dogmatic and irrational a redemption as the Church laid down.

This is the state of affairs to-day in Catholic Europe regarding the intolerable dogmatism of the Roman Church. The history of it all is in the Pope's recent encyclical. Read between the lines, and you become aware that a battle royal is being waged between an irrational, spiritless, tho unyielding antiquarianism, and a thinking, spiritual, and suppliant modernism. Who would dare dream of the modern attitude in the Roman Church? Yet there it is, and whether or not to stay, it is troubling the placid waters from their most secret center to their farthest shores. Let Pius X. define the issue. "Every modernist," he exclaims, "comprizes within himself many personalities; he is a philosopher, a believer, a theologian, a historian, a critic, an apologist, and a reformer."[1] My! what wealth of faith, scholarship, culture, zeal for truth, spiritual excellence is embraced in any man who can fill so many honorable offices! How valuable to any church! But alas! not if your church be unphilosophical, unbelieving, noncritical, non-apologetic, and neither historical nor theological in any truly scientific fashion. Therefore we can see why the assumed successor of St. Peter refers to them thus: "They are striving by arts entirely new and full of subtlety to destroy the vital energy of the Church; . . . they are enemies of the Church. . . . They are the most pernicious of all the adversaries of the Church. . . .

[1] Dr. Newman Smyth, "Passing Protestantism and Coming Catholicism," p. 45.

[30]

They put their designs for her ruin into operation not from without but from within, hence
the danger is present almost in the very veins
and heart of the Church.''

Now I am sure we want to know who these
piratical, even anarchistic fellows may be who
are, as was their divine Master two thousand
years ago, accused of perverting the nation.
Well, there is Father Tyrrell in England, who
is spoken of by an impartial biographer ''as
a servant elect of God, filled with searching
honesty of thought, and consuming flame of
spirit. He has been suspended from priestly
office because he has discovered for himself
the Christ, and henceforth would confess the
foundation faith which flesh and blood have
not revealed to him.''

There is also Abbé Loisy, professor of New
Testament interpretation in what is perhaps
Rome's chief school of training, the Sor-
bonne, France, whose classroom is so
thronged with students for the priesthood
that it is always overflowing into the corridors. He is described as an impartial investigator, learned interpreter of the Scriptures,
keen critic, and believer in the guidance of

the Holy Spirit. His benign smile impresses all who observe him. "Oh! that smile of the Abbé Loisy! Whoever has seen it will never forget it. It is not the smile of a malicious person who banters or jeers; it is not the smile of a pedant who scoffs; it is not the smile of a dissenter who is proud of his dissent; it is the smile of a reasonable man who exercises his reason and who does so for the pleasure of exercising it, because that exercise is properly the end, the essential function of life, because we are in this world to act with reason." [1]

Another leader of modernism is Senator Fogazzaro, whose famous religious novel, "The Saint," is regarded to be the "Uncle Tom's Cabin" of the reform movement in the Roman Church. Needless to say his book has been put under the Church's anathema, and all loyal Catholics forbidden to read it. Why? Because Fogazzaro affirms that religion is not ecclesiasticism nor an authorized mass of beliefs, even tho supposed to come down from the apostles, but that it is, above all, action and life. He puts the practise of

[1] "Passing Protestantism and Coming Catholicism," p. 58.

the gospel ahead of intellectual religious action even, and declares that love comes before faith." [1]

And hear the declaration of Don Romolo Murri, who commands a large and devoted following in the Italian Church: "Priest I am, priest I remain, respectful of authority, faithful to my duties, and I feel in myself the painful conflict which at this hour of profound crisis agitates Catholicism. . . . The cause of it all lies in the lack of real religion. The principal cause of it belongs to those priests who represent reaction. . . . We desire a Christianity more pure, more intense, more practical, more Christian, more conformed to its original, more conformed to the gospel."

How splendid a creed is that! What Christlike spirit it embodies! Yet these heroes, mighty in spirit and thought, are called enemies of the Church, most pernicious adversaries, accurst for all time because they are historians, philosophers, believers, reformers, believing in and teaching two doctrines essential to the existence of Christianity and the vitality of the Church;

[1] "Passing Protestantism and Coming Catholicism," p. 62.

namely, "the immanence of God in man, and the permanent presence of Christ in the Church."[1] Such is what the pope condemns as agnosticism. Let Christendom decide if this statement be agnosticism or precious certitude of faith, "The profound conviction by which all our actions are inspired is God in Christ and Christ in the Church."

Why I dwell at length on this spiritual movement in the Roman Church is because it has within it the promise of a second Reformation, and the names of Tyrrell, Loisy, Murri, Fogazzaro may become as world-famed as those of Luther, Melanchthon, and Erasmus. In fact, Pius X. says in his encyclical that "modernism leads to the annihilation of all religion. The first step in this direction was Protestantism, the second is made by modernism; the next will plunge headlong into atheism."[2] The head of the Church here makes modernism a second Reformation, but virtually calls Protestantism, modernism, and atheism the trinity of the Roman anathema.

To think is the great curse in Rome's

[1] "Passing Protestantism and Coming Catholicism," p. 78.
[2] *Ibid.*, pp. 47, 48.

ecclesiasticism. Reason, religious freedom, the sanctity of the individual conscience have no standing, win no respect, merit no tolerance. The light must be kept out at all hazards.

Lamentable as is such an attitude in the Roman Catholic Church, it is more so a thousandfold in the Protestant, for our very birth was a protest against such unscriptural dogma and irrational authority. Therefore our existence to be valid must stand up forever against all traditionalism of Scripture, of creed, of ecclesiastical organization that will not brook revision, the advice of devout scholarship, the convictions of reason and of the spiritual consciousness of man.

Let Doctor Gordon again speak on this very point in the sermon already referred to: "The world of science is undergoing constant revision and expansion; new facts and new ideas in every department of science are the continuous surprise of the time; the hope of fresh discovery in fact and in law is the perpetual incentive of the scientific mind. History is rewritten in every new century out of larger knowledge and wider vistas of man's world.

[35]

Philosophy, the world of man's deepest thoughts, is in continual movement, and the sympathetic man discovers in this movement the possibility, at least, of a richer and vaster issue. Religion is a living experience, and among thoughtful men it must seek to bring itself into accord with general knowledge about man's world. Religion as feeling and character is growing, is bound to grow wherever it is alive. Religion as insight into the ultimate meanings of existence and the universe is also bound to grow where the religious intellect is not the victim of despair. Under all aspects, our human world is provisional, incomplete, awaiting revision and expansion. How shall we behave toward this our world thus freed from servitude? Believe that the spirit of truth is in the intellect and will of the world. Believe that all attested truth in science is one with all essential truth in religion."[1]

Doctor Gordon laments that such freedom for the truth is not yet. Doctor Smyth laments it so hopelessly that he claims Protestantism

[1] Dr. George Gordon, "The Progressive Revelation of Truth," Sermon in *Congregationalist*, July 11, 1908.

is gradually ceasing to be regarded as a final
and permanent condition of religious thought.
"Its great work is achieved, its victory won
forever for the spiritual liberty of the individual man."[1]

Smyth further sees Protestantism's work
completed because for two hundred years it
has not been much occupied in making new
denominations or in devising new formulas
of faith; on the other hand, it has been breaking up rather than making creeds. Therefore
both the age of protest and reconstruction is
gone.[2]

"Protestantism has, furthermore, lost authority over human life, as represented in the
community and the family, wherein anything
and everything is the master passion save religion.[3] It has lost influence over vast areas
of thought, religious education is null, religious thinking in pulpit and pew is a lost art."[4]

Besides all this incalculable loss, Doctor
Smyth laments "that the contact is broken between the current of thought in the Church

[1] Dr. Smyth, "Passing Protestantism and Coming Catholicism," p. 10.
[2] *Ibid.*, p. 8.   [3] *Ibid*, pp. 14 and 15.   [4] *Ibid.*, p. 19.

and the general mental activity of the day."[1] He asserts that "Protestantism does not attract thinking men, and Rome repels them."[2]

"A further inefficiency," he claims, "results from a divided Christianity as manifested in denominationalism, also in lack of unity in the denomination."[3]

These strictures furnish food for serious thought. Every one of them contains more truth than we all are ready to admit, but which few of us would feel qualified to deny. Whether they and other possible signs of a completed work and relinquished mastery point away to another name and form for the conserving of our faith only the future can reveal. But of this much we can be very confident, whether it be the name Protestantism or Catholicism that designates the religious body universal, nevertheless it will be Christian. Christ will be enthroned in the midst. While the religious pendulum is swinging between a supposed decadent Protestantism and a (as yet) still-born and quite unformed

[1] Smyth, p. 20.　　　　[2] *Ibid.*, p. 21.
[3] *Ibid.*, pp. 23-25.

Catholicism, let us remember that there is something here now of more divine potency and significance than either Protestantism or Catholicism. It is Christianity. It is the teaching and spirit of Christ that have come down from Bethlehem and Jerusalem, from the manger and the cross, irradiating with divinest light and filling with purest spirit the minds and hearts of men. "The wind bloweth where it listeth, and thou hearest the sound thereof, but canst not tell whence it cometh or whither it goeth, so is every one that is born of the Spirit."

Protestantism's work completed, why not let Christianity's work begin, as formless, nameless, and creedless as in the simple days of Galilee, but withal as powerful? If creeds are breaking instead of making, why not see those breaks to be a providential stage in the history of Christianity for the incoming tides of the Spirit? If Protestantism does not attract thinking men and Rome repels them, let us not concede the only alternative to be infidelity. Why not Christianity as an alternative? The gospel has always large drawing power. Easier to find out what it is, incorporate some of its available supply into a decadent Protestantism, and the rest of it into life and action, than to cast about for a new and more universal form of procedure and appreciation. And if Protestantism has lost control of things in both the communal and domestic realms, pray let Christianity become the regulator and authority there. The pierced hand upon the helm of human actuality and destiny will speedily and marvelously adjust things to God's liking and man's good.

The saddest part of all Smyth's lamentable state of affairs is, perhaps, the part to which this statement refers, that the contact is broken between the current of thought in the Church and the general mental activity of the day. We all have seen and felt the evidences of this. It is a somewhat wide-spread phenomenon that collegiate and professionally educated young men and women are not church-going young men and women; few young men, even tho devoutly Christian, go into the ministry. It is not that our universities teach unbelief in the Church, the Scriptures, the Christ. University influence and precept in

America are strongly the other way. May not the reason be that the university provides so satisfactory a religious substitute? A substitute freed from gloomy dogmatism and rigorous creed and trammeling sectarianism, but with the refreshments of simplicity, rationality, tolerance, and a delicious attractiveness characterizing it all. I fear this is at least part of the cause, the other part being that when the youth is let go by the university, he fails to return to the formal, sometimes unthinking, often unspiritual ministrations of the Church.

Coincident with this loss of control over the thought of the age, Doctor Smyth sees a strange happening, but not so strange but that other eyes observe. It is that much religion is withdrawing from the churches. "In almost any community," he continues, "there may be found considerable numbers of people who are not in their habit of mind irreligious, nor without faith in their hearts. But they belong to no Church, confess no creed, and rarely attend public worship. There is a kind of religious literature not generally known among our church membership, seldom recognized by theologians, but to be found in the book-stores, and having large sales among such persons outside our communions, a literature that is somewhat mystical, quietistic, and spiritual, but neither churchly nor very distinctively Christian. The spread of this kind of literature outside the domain of the Church is a noteworthy phenomenon. The older mysticism, the former quietism flourished within the Church. Now it springs up largely outside the churches and beyond their creeds."[1]

Such is no insignificant sign of the times. Dr. Worcester exclaims in the book "Religion and Medicine," and in his chapter upon the outlook of the Church: "Many are deterred from entering the Church by honest intellectual scruples and difficulties, and for these the Church has a heavy responsibility. But it is safe to say if the Church, which is the natural home of the Christian religion, declines while humanity progresses, such a decline can have but one cause; namely, that the Church is not doing her whole duty. A large and ever-increasing number of intelligent persons feel

[1] Smyth, pp. 17 and 18.

that the Church has outgrown or is outgrowing her usefulness. Why do they feel this? Because the Church is no longer indispensable to men. Unquestionably one of the great motives of all human belief is the practical motive—believing because it is good and useful to believe. The good religion has done the world and is still doing is one of the chief reasons man believes in religion; and the more good any particular religion or church is able to do, the more men will believe in it, and the less visible good the Church does the less men will believe in it."[1]

It was the consciousness of this loosing of the ecclesiastical bond upon the communal and individual life that incited the remark earlier in the chapter that the present spiritual tendency of the Church can be better stated in negative than positive terms, and that its relinquishments of what is not conducive to the life of the spirit is more apparent than its achievements in that life. The loosing of the hold has opened the way for a more spiritual and practical content through which the Church's hand can be strengthened to take

[1] Doctor Worcester "Religion and Medicine," p. 370.

fresh, firm hold again, and become filled with profitable inducement for the labor-wearied, pleasure-surfeited, sin-sick men and women of the world to come in and find divine uplift, intellectual comfort, a larger degree of physical and spiritual completeness. Smyth says: "Experimental science has driven out abstract dogmatism. Eventually scholastic systems of divinity must give way to the religion of experience."[1]

So it must, and it is. What else can be the meaning of that cry that has been ringing in the ears of Church and world for a decade or more, "Back to Christ?" Never in the history of Christian aspiration has there been a larger appreciation of the New Testament and apostolic power of Christianity to satisfy the entire sphere of human need. Nor could we, in all the world's history, go back to Christ so intelligently. The devout critical examination of the Scriptures has magnified and not detracted from the real Christ. The scientific principle of evolution, with its necessary biological connections, has shown the need of

[1] Smyth, p. 97.

spiritual connections also, that the life system present a completed whole. The new psychologic knowledge that has opened up such far-reaching remedial possibilities in the human mind, and suggests such profound power throughout the entire universe, needs the assurances of Christianity, and the revelations of the Spirit, but of a simple, reasonable, undogmatic, unecclesiastical kind. The multitudinous miscellaneous literature of "somewhat mystical, quietistic, and spiritual, but neither churchly nor very distinctly Christian nature," shows whither the mind and heart of man are turning for spiritual food. These tendencies are more truly pointing back to Christ than are some of the well-organized departments of our Protestant faith.

These forces are reconstructive also. They are some of the chracteristics of Protestant modernism that are asking to be housed inside the Church. The question is if the Church will take advantage of the opportunity to be abreast of the age by its incorporation of the full gospel of the Son of Man, and by extending abiding entertainment unto all modern reconstructive forces

that through their earnest, truth-loving attitudes are humbly or devoutly asking for the
Church's adoption, unto the regaining of its
lost prestige with the common life and the existing of a more completely remedial leaven-
ing of the human lump than at any time since
the third century of the Christian era.

Protestantism, it is safe to say, will not
repudiate these modernists as Roman Catholicism has done. Why should it, with nothing to lose and everything to gain, even its
very life to conserve? It has no single anti-
quated position of the Roman dogmatism to
safeguard and perpetuate. It is instead a
protest against it all. We are told that its
greatest achievement is the spiritual liberty
of the individual. That achievement, however much it has meant in the past, must
mean no less in the present and future. The
individual's spiritual liberties must be as
sacred and dear to the twentieth as they were
to the sixteenth-century Church.

Lest some critical reader wonder that no
mention is made in this introductory chapter of that Christian altruism that must be
exprest in social service if the Church is to

keep abreast of the times, a question of such
prominence that already the Church has been
called upon by some of our noblest scholars
to adjust itself to the social demand, I would
assure such reader of my heartiest appreciation of such Christ-sanctioned endeavor;
and go so far as to express perfect accord
with such exposition of the social problem
and the organic Christian relation thereto as
is exprest in Professor Matthews' "The
Church and the Changing Order," Professor
Leighton's "Jesus Christ and the Civilization of To-day," and that strong work of my
much-respected teacher Professor Peabody,
"Jesus Christ and 'the Social Question."
What Professor Matthews states about the
relation of the Church toward life in general,
especially the life of social service, is worthy
of quotation not only as reenforcement for
the positions taken in this chapter, but also
for his own splendid contention "that the
Church must face the vital decision as to
what part it shall have in producing the new
world."[1] "This is the real crisis of the

[1] Professor Matthews, "The Church and the Changing
Order," p. 3.

Church, the need that it define its attitude toward formative forces now at work. Will it move on indifferent to their existence, or will it cooperate with them, correct them, inspire them with its own ideals and insure that their results shall insure a better to-morrow? A new age is immanent. Will the Church guarantee that it shall be in no narrow individualistic way Christian?"[1] Professor Matthews is quite correct when he exclaims that "a spreading materialism should teach the Church that men want something more than abstract virtue or transcendental ethics,"[2] also in his contention that "Our civilization is threatened with an ethical materialism." But it is also threatened with a certain Christian mysticism that is allying itself with certain scientifically demonstrated modern psychologic principles which, if the Church does not "correct and also inspire with its own ideals," will make for a completer disintegration of its influence than is at present realized.

Professor Matthews states "that the greatest formative principle in the world of

[1] Matthews, p. 6.   [2] *Ibid.*, pp. 214 and 215.

[48]

thought to-day is biology.'' [1] That statement is much truer than the Church believes. But there is just one formative principle that is greater than this greatest. That is Christianity, of a simple, practical, undogmatic, unsectarian kind; and being employed as a precious health-saving, mind-inspiring, spirit-sobering truth. But it is waiting to be corrected and legalized by the Church's methods and standards.

The Emmanuel movement, so-called, is a serious and successful attempt at this correction and legalizing. It embodies within its concept the most modern scientific principles, biological, psychological, theological, and in the interpretation of the Scriptures. In this embodiment is also represented what it believes to be Christ's intention regarding the entire man; namely, that he be possest of bodily strength as truly as of spiritual zeal that he may the better fill out his destiny, and the more worthily honor his God. Chapters nine and ten set forth more definitely than this introductory chapter can attempt what the writer understands the Emmanuel

[1] Matthews, p. 28.

movement to be, and the remedial work it is able to perform. The official book of the Emmanuel movement, "Religion and Medicine," edited by three of the Emmanuel Church staff, Boston, where the movement originated—Doctors Worcester, McComb and Coriat—contains all necessary elucidation of the more technical side of the principles involved, as well as reference to the curative work that has been achieved.

This volume—"Mind, Religion and Health" —it should be stated, is virtually a book of sermons. All the chapters have been more or less changed, especially the first, fourth, seventh, ninth, eleventh and twelfth, which have been somewhat lengthened. It might be well to say the last four chapters were preached as sermons first, then the first eight, the entire twelve chapters being given to the public upon twelve consecutive Sabbath evenings. The first eight sermons were preached by request of many who asked to be told how the remedial principles outlined in the little series of four sermons descriptive of the Emmanuel movement could be practised in the daily life.

When these two series of sermons were prepared there was no thought of putting them in book form. This has been done to satisfy a far-reaching demand. The interest in this new health movement seems nothing short of phenomenal throughout the country. This statement is based upon the hundreds of letters that have been received by the author from all over the United States, and from all sorts and conditions of men. Clergymen, physicians, would-be patients, suffering from all conceivable maladies, have asked for information upon the principles of this movement. They desired such information as would enable them to take advantage of its health-producing powers; clergymen for their congregations, physicians for their patients, the people at large, both in and out of health, that the happiness of their lives and homes be safeguarded and increased.

Moreover, it was complained that there was little or no published information to be secured. This is not strange, considering the newness of the movement. It is to meet this universal demand on the part of earnest people, as well as to satisfy the desire of would-be benefactors of humanity in the largest and most practical sense possible, that this book is given to the public. It is an endeavor to help both those who are seeking health as well as those who, possessing it, desire to retain it.

It has been thought well to incorporate some questions and answers bearing on points in the sermons concerning which more light was desired. These questions and answers should not be overlooked by those who are interested in mental and religious therapeutics. Especially should they be read by those who are desirous to know what the author conceives the scope of the Emmanuel movement to be, inasmuch as they sum up in concise form important beliefs and conclusions regarding psychotherapeutics.

I

THE MIND'S POWER OVER OUR ILLS

As a man thinketh in his heart so is he.—OLD TESTA-
MENT SCRIPTURES.

Let this mind be in you which was also in Christ Jesus.—
NEW TESTAMENT SCRIPTURES.

The one thing in the world of value is the active soul.
—RALPH WALDO EMERSON.

*Our own spirit is the vestibule which we must enter, as
threshold to the temple of the eternal, and wherein alone we
can catch any whisper from the Holy of Holies.*
—JAMES MARTINEAU.

*A mind not to be changed by place or time. . . . .
. . . . . And in itself can make a heaven of hell, a hell
of heaven.*
—MILTON.

*Our remedies oft in ourselves do lie, which we ascribe to
Heaven.*
—SHAKESPEARE.

*No scientist will deny the existence within us of a central
intelligence which controls the bodily functions, and through
the sympathetic nervous system actuates the involuntary
muscles and keeps the bodily machinery in motion. Nor
will the most pronounced materialist deny that this central
intelligence is the controlling energy which regulates the
action of each of the myriad cellular entities of which the
whole body is composed.*
—HUDSON.

I

THE MIND'S POWER OVER OUR ILLS

Views of medical authorities upon the necessity for psychological treatment in behalf of a large number of physical maladies—What experience shows concerning mental control—Illustrations from nature and art of both divine and human interference with the uniformity of nature—the value of the mind of Christ—How it imparts the God-consciousness in the place of self-consciousness—How it lifts us from the superficial to the real; enabling us to live in the sunshine—How it builds for us a new-world order which is permeated by an atmosphere of purity and health.

NEVER before in the history of the world have the physician of the body and the physician of the soul been more intelligently at one. This has been brought about by the conviction that each has to do with the other's sphere of usefulness. The Church no longer ministers to the mind and ignores the body. The medical practitioner no longer treats the body and ignores the mind. Both are heeding the divine call as never before to attend to the necessities of the entire man. From the religious side this has been going on some time. The so-called institutional church, with gymnasium, employment bureau, reading-room, citizenship league, and industrial department to teach poor girls cooking, sewing, millinery, and general housekeeping, and poor boys competency in the trades and arts, is a recognition of the call. And the Emmanuel movement, which is a rational establishing on scriptural grounds of the many heretofore sporadic attempts within the Church and without to banish certain grievous ills, carries this desire to remedy the whole man into the physical realm with amazingly beneficial results.

On the other hand, the medical profession is awakening to a new responsibility, tho some of the best physicians took it up long ago; namely, to use all psychic and natural forces as curative power for diseases beyond the reach of drugs and surgery. Dr. Schofield, of the British Medical Association, whose illuminating work ''The Mental Factor in Medicine'' should be in every home, claims that philosophy, theology, and medicine touch each other, and that there is a transition ground that is common to all. "On this ground," he continues, "the physician should stand with as much authority as the priest and philosopher." "The Church," he exclaims, "no longer treats the soul and ignores the man, but the care of the human being as a whole, soul and body, is increasingly coming to the front. And in the same way the wise physician must grasp the underlying unity of the spiritual and the material, and recognize that if the body may and does influence diseases of the soul, so does the mind influence states and diseases of the body." "I utterly refuse," he continues, "to regard the mental factor in medicine as a retrogression. It is, on the contrary, a step, and a great step, in advance, for the day is past when the physician can limit his knowledge and practise by the physical."

In another place Dr. Schofield states: "I remember when addressing the London clergy on behalf of the National Health Society, impressing upon them that if the physician can not fully treat the body without any reference to the spirit, neither can the clergy care for the soul without regard for the body. Considerable impatience was shown by my audience at my spending time to elaborate a point which to them seemed so obvious, and afterward they told me the day was past when the conception of Christianity was limited to the soul.''

Dr. Laycock, an eminent English physician, claims that the most eminent and successful physicians have all been psychologists, for the knowledge of a practical science of mind is fundamentally necessary to the practise of medicine. Professor Gardiner, president of the British Medical Society, says ''we must acknowledge that the spiritual element in man is brought necessarily into the sphere of the physician's work.'' De Fleury says ''the modern doctor must understand the pathology and hygiene of the intellect. But the fields of psycho-physiology and psycho-therapeutics are as yet almost untouched.'' Professor Ladd, in an article in the *Medical Times,* says: ''The effects capable of being produced by mind on body are very clear, real and considerable, and while in all ages they have been the chief therapeutic agents on which the charlatan and quack have relied, they have probably been less trusted and utilized by the scientific physician than experience warrants or psychology suggests." Professor Clouston says: "We talk and laugh and weep and blush and shiver and hunger and sweat and digest all through the brain cortex, and there is not one of the physiological acts but can be instantly arrested by a mental act."

Dr. Schofield brings to a close this convincing array of authorities with the statement that when we once grasp the interaction of mind and body in health we are better prepared to understand the part they play in disease and cure. He continues: "By conscious action the heart's action can be slowed, and even arrested." In continuance of this idea is the statement of Dr. Reinne of London that the sudden emotion of fear or pleasure upon the heart may produce palpitation, actual contraction, and even death. And Dr. Morton Prince, of Boston, contributes a humorous statement of a lady who always had a violent attack of hay-fever when a rose was in the room. One day he brought in an artificial rose and the usual symptoms followed. He then showed her it was made of paper and had no pollen, and ever after all symptoms disappeared. And may I quote Dr. Schofield once again, who tells of a man who came to him for a cure from dyspepsia and general debility, but finding he had defrauded his brother, he advised him to repay, and immediately the case was cured.

I have on my desk twenty medical authorities other than those referred to showing that many organic as well as functional diseases are caused by mental and emotional conditions. The list includes diabetes, angina pectoris, apoplexy, asthma, dyspepsia, liver trouble, epilepsy, tumors, and cancers. Sir B. W. Richardson claims that diabetes is undoubtedly caused by mental strain. Sir George Paget claims that in many cases cancer has its origin in prolonged anxiety. Dr. Snow, Dr. Murchison, and Sir W. H. Bennett of St. George's Hospital, London, all agree that cancer of the liver, the breast, the uterus, are due to mental anxiety.

Such being true, it behooves us to realize that ''as a man thinketh in his heart, so is

[60]

he," which text, by the way, was given me by a Brooklyn physician of highest standing. Such being true, it were well to have in us the mind which was also in Christ Jesus. For remember that it is an established principle in medical science that diseases caused by deranged mental and moral conditions can be remedied and even cured by healthful mental and moral force. Dr. Schofield exclaims that force of mind is a health-producing agent in every disease. Dr. Dubois of Germany exclaims that nervousness is a disease preeminently psychic, and a psychic disease needs psychic treatment. Then he asks this question: "Can we by means of the mind, by our moral deportment, escape illness, prevent functional troubles, diminish or suppress those which already exist? I boldly answer, yes." And hear this startling statement from Dr. Schofield: "The power of mind over the body has limits, but they have never yet been ascertained. All one can do to cure himself, the forces he can set in action, are as yet unknown, but they are far greater than most people imagine."

In coming years we will hear less about the

uniformity of nature and more about the remedial redemptive forces of the psychic life. Concerning the therapeutic agencies for both body and soul there has been too much emphasis upon materia-medica for the one, and a materia-religia for the other. But now the way is open for the introduction of those mental and spiritual forces, heretofore unrelied on, but always here, and tho unrecognized and unnamed, doing their redemptive work. Just as there was no room for Jesus at the inn on that glad morning of the advent, but now at home in lordly mansion and in palace hall, so the coming of God, unto all immanence, into these bodily mansions where sits enthroned the most divine of all creations—the soul—marks a new era in the content of our faith. The rationalizing of life to the exclusion of the mystical elements that are at the core of religion can not go unchecked for long. The spiritual instincts, and the psychic claims of the religious believer must be respected. Whatever may be agreed upon as forming the constituency of religion, be it the feeling of absolute dependence as Schleiermacher would have it, or that of guilt and the divine forgiveness as Jonathan Edwards conceived, or that of the consciousness of the divine love, and an answering childlike trust in the All Father, as Channing claimed, nevertheless the essential oneness of the finite spirit with the Infinite Spirit must be conceded. That concession once made, nature's uniformity becomes in our thought less mechanical and unyielding; the miraculous interposition of the Supreme Intelligence that gave nature existence becomes less miraculous; reason becomes more friendly to the presence of the spiritual; and religious faith becomes more rational and sane.

While that blessed day star dawneth, it shineth dimly as yet. The rationalist still exclaims how irrational and unscientific is the religionist, and we religionists exclaim how irrational is rationality. While their contention is undoubtedly real to them, ours is extremely realistic to us. See this deplorable condition spelled out in striking detail.

The intellectualist, especially he of scientific cast of mind who rationalizes everything, or thinks he does, and boasts he will not believe in what he can not understand, repudiates the miraculous element in Christianity because it makes inroads upon the uniformity of nature. But what is the miraculous if not the incoming of the Infinite Intelligence in unforeseen, unexperienced manner to make all things new. What is nature for but to have its uniformity broken up in behalf of some divinely designful, transforming, transfiguring improvement or other. To what better advantage can it be put than to furnish material for finished product, when the All-creative mind would achieve the higher utilities. Nature exists then not so much to have its regularity conserved as to become a point of departure for all designful construction.

The scientific objector to the divine interference with nature's order of procedure denies God the privilege he himself is all the while assuming in every realization of the good, the beautiful, the true. Human thought never wearies in transforming the natural and physical. All labor, skill, manifestation of genius is human thought exercised on raw material for worthy use. The table I write on is the oak-tree plus an interposition of mind. The pen I use is crude steel uniformly square, round or flat until thought thins, curves and sharpens it. Put thought into the wild rose and you have the crimson rambler and American beauty. Put it into the wayside apple, sour and bitter, and the luscious pippin or gravenstein is yours to enjoy. Put it into the untamed steed of the prairie, and you have the Morgan thoroughbred. No royal vase, as valuable perhaps as a King's crown, could be molded without the common clay being stamped, in its every atom with human thought. The clay was valueless. The vase, the value of rubies. The factor in which all the value resides is the thought that transformed and transfigured the clay.

Handel was a failure at writing operas. His thought was too fine and serious. Longing for worthier vehicle of expression he, one day, picked up a leaf of the New Testament from the floor of the room in Dublin where he was visiting a friend. It contained the story of Christ's crucifixion. He set his mind upon that priceless tattered leaf, and "The Messiah" sprang into being for the delight of the entire musical world. Raphael in a wise moment picked up a barrel-head. Through his brushes and paints, both of which were of trifling cost, he spread his thoughts over it. The result was that priceless Madonna of the Chair, which is worth many, many times its weight in gold. Phidias broke up the uniformity of one of the Pentelic marble quarries, set Ictinus and Callicrates to work chiseling his multitudinous thought images into it, and the Greek Parthenon, with its 228 by 102 feet of solid thought design, sprang forth to rejoice all ancient and astonish all modern mortals. The grandeur of Saint Peter's is only the stone-clothed art-preserved thinking of Michelangelo, who gladly toiled seventeen years without pay, to save his soul he said; rather to help redeem each inconspicuous soul in all the ages who might chance to gaze upon that monument to Michelangelo's immortal thought. Such also is the history of his Pieta, just an incrusted, sculptured thought, but so powerful and true withal as to make a youth of twenty summers the first artist in Italy. So is the Marble Faun the mind of Praxiteles embodied in outer form for our admiration. And Hamlet and Othello the mind of Shakespeare toying with pen, ink and paper to astonish the world.

There is no constructive agency in the entire universe save mind. Whether it manifest itself orderly through law, or spontaneously in unforeseen fashion, it ever remains the one all-marvelous, all-comprehending entity in existence. The material side of things is the lifeless side, having value only as it furnishes occasion and form for the designs and embodiments of the mind's untiring endeavor. The body takes its form and substance from the soul. It is that psychic dynamic incentive, constituting us men, that produces all bodily motion. The kind of psychic force within determines the clumsiness or grace of each outer act and motion. Swedenborg declares "that the human body with all its parts and functions is elaborated from the soul, therefore corresponds to it in every particular of structure, form and use." Herbert Spencer speaks of the eternal energy whence all things proceed and by which all organisms are constructed.. Emerson exclaims "that the great men are they who see

[67]

that spiritual is stronger than material force, that thoughts rule the world.''

The only way possible for invisible forces to become manifest, if ever known at all, is through material forms and terms such as motion, color, sound. Then, and not before, our senses take them in. All philosophy other than sheer materialism goes back to Plato's invisible world of ideas that are in one or another way translated in phenomena. Thus everything that is seen is an incarnation of what is not seen. The seen, the touched, the measurable, the ponderable, are the cruder vibrations—the garment, as it were, of the unseen, the immeasurable, the spiritual.

Dr. John Hunter, the eminent surgeon, and the no less-renowned Johann Mueller testify that any mental state may be induced in any part of the body by constant attention and serious intention. We can demonstrate this for ourselves in relation to temperature and the flow of blood to certain bodily parts, even to the rising of the mercury in a spirit thermometer held in the closed hand with the thought intensely turned thereon. It is surely not going too far to affirm that the mind builds up the body or tears it down, changing it at will in conformity with its truth convictions, else its hallucinations of worry and fear. The medical authorities are legion who concede that the heart's action can be quickened or slowed, and that instantly, by both our conscious and unconscious mental processes. So can the pulse be quickened or retarded; the action of the intestines stimulated, abdominal pains alleviated; perspiration induced; dyspepsia cured; the cheek reddened with blood, else paled with sickly deathlike pallor. Who has not seen the maiden's face time and again flush with blushes at a word or look? Who has not felt his own assume this telltale appearance in an embarrassed moment?

Some one has said that the face is the titlepage of the soul, with the contents of the volume inscribed thereon. How true. Our face is the unerring index of the inner life. A passing glance shows whether there be animalistic or moral dominance within, serious or flippant motive, pure or sensuous feeling, dutiful or selfish inclinations, cultured or coarse-grained thought. We will never outgrow the truth of the old adage that beauty is more than skin deep. The amber, saffron and crimson hues on the skin of apple and peach are core deep, inwrought into their very seed. So lie all sources of beauty close packed in the soul. Fair complexions can't be bought. Only the fool thinks they reside in cosmetics, powders and rouge. The kind of daily attention one should give face and body are not of that, nor of any such superficial care.

But why multiply authorities? Why cite manifold illustrations? Do we not intuitively know that the mind and the self are identical? That man is a soul and has a body, which is as a tenement in which he is dwelling for a while until God calls him unto a purely spiritual abode? Surely we have become convinced that possessing the mind in purity— the purity of faith, reverence, hope and love, and always keeping it at its best—we possess everything worth having. While if we have neglected its culture and allowed it to become weakened and diseased all that concerns us becomes sickly and impoverished in consequence. O brother, do not underestimate the value of the mind, but keep it so strong and rich and healthful that no diseased fancies can lodge there, no sickly thoughts steal in, no harmful vicious intruders trespass, and with their base insinuations soil and debase its sanctity. All you possess, that wealth you strove to accumulate has value only as you have a mind to appreciate it, else it is so much useless waste. Be warned to guard your mind even more tenderly than you would the apple of your eye. Shakespeare said in the "Taming of the Shrew," " 'Tis the mind that makes the body rich." The great Pascal said: "Man is greater than the universe because he can pass in thought from star to star, from moon to sun, and yet no star nor moon nor sun can follow him." Isaac Watts, who was deformed, said: "Were I so tall to reach the pole, or grasp the ocean with a span, I must be measured by my soul. The mind's the standard of the man." Yes, yes, it is true, I must be measured by my soul.

God's universe is to every man exactly what his mind sees it to be. If the mind be free, and light, and joyous, the world is ablaze with sunlight, joy, and happiness, even tho in appearance it be the darkest day of all the year. But if sorrow and despair have found lodgment there the world's delights and grand activities are huge mountains of dreariness in which is no fascination at all, but intensest weariness instead. Develop the mind by educational processes and the universe is no longer the shallow thing it was before, but a profound aggregate of cause and effect, of mysterious laws and forces, of deepest, grandest purposes and design. Instil lustful thoughts into it, and a world of animalism results. While if spiritual thoughts hold possession, and the mind endures as seeing Him who is invisible, the world's barren waste becomes a paradise again.

O the power of the mind to control the life. I had a friend once who played false, deliberately and desperately, with this magnificent trust of life the wise Creator has entrusted to us all, and wearied with the strife he plunged himself into a suicide's grave. Was the world the disagreeable place he thought it? No. Was public opinion

against him as he imagined? No. Were his
employers dissatisfied and plotting to take
from him his occupation and his bread? No.
His employers loved him as a son. His towns-
men were his friends. Everybody spoke well
of him and no one ill. And as for the world,
there never was a sunnier day than that on
which the foul deed was done. It was the
mind that controlled the life. The day was
dark to him for he saw it to be dark. His
employers were against him because he
thought them so. Public opinion pointed at
him in scorn because the mind where sweet
contentment should have reigned, and love of
wife and child, and the respect of the community and the fair light of God's face was
morbid and diseased. Distorted images
stalked there. Strange hallucinations held
the mind in check, and at their heels prest
the demons of despair and seized the citadel.
Friends talked with him and tried to explain
away his wrong ideas, but it is as Froude, the
historian said: "When a man is possest of a
strong idea and a wrong idea he can not be
reasoned with." The poet Shelley's despairing man comes to our thought: "Come near

and help me. I weave a chain I can not break. I am possest with thoughts too swift and strong for one lone human breast.''

The mind must be fortified against despondency. High thoughts, rich thoughts, must be instilled. It must be filled so full and with so many that all lower thoughts be crowded out, else kept in the minority, the hopeless minority, so far as influencing the life is concerned.

The apostle takes radical ground just here. ''Let this mind be in you which was also in Christ Jesus''—a mind thoroughly identified with the world's sorrows, but never made despondent by grief and bitterness, and no weariness of life followed in their wake. Be sure it depends upon the kind of a mind you have, what your life shall be, and how the world shall look. A material mind, which is that of the majority of men, loves material things above all else, and if it fails to gain these it becomes of all minds most miserable. An intellectual mind, that of a Darwin, a Spencer, a Huxley, a Carlyle, loves intellectual acquisition above all, and nothing can, it thinks, compensate for the loss of that. A

spiritual mind, that of a Luther, a Savo-
narola, a Wesley, a Moody, a Phillips Brooks,
cares little whether business is good or bad,
whether stocks are up or down, whether the
banks are paying three per cent or ten.

O the uplift to the mind of Christ for it
fills us with the consciousness of God's presence. Therein is the preventive and curative
power for disease. Man's greatest curse is
self-consciousness when it is allowed to be a
barrier to God. All sin springs from that
limitation. Sensitiveness, enviousness, hatred, nervousness, worry, melancholy, hysteria, all have their rootage there. It is self-
consciousness that makes, what Dr. Weir
Mitchell calls the whole man, ill.

> Our best have owned the rare dramatic power,
> Which gives to sympathy its lifting power.
> Go learn of them, the masters of our art,
> To trust that wise consultant called the heart.
> There are among us those who haply please
> To think our business is to treat disease
> And all unknowing lack this lesson still—
> 'Tis not the body, but the man that's ill.

Self-consciousness makes the whole man
ill. God-consciousness makes the whole man

well. The one is being tied up to the world with its friction, its worry, its stultification, its disease and death. The other opens us up to the universal, the eternal, filling us with a sense of its largeness and buoyancy, wherein is all good cheer and health. The one shuts us up in the cellar of our discontent where the outlook is dark, the air foul, the surroundings depressing. The other allows us to inhabit the highest, sunniest chamber of the soul, into which flash vitality, and the inspirations of God, that can be carried down through every nerve, muscle, and tissue of our physical frame.

Again the mind of Christ places and keeps us on the heights, lifting our consciousness from the seen to the unseen, and opening all our little restricted nature to the joyous rhythm of the universal life. What cowards we are when dominated by the seen. We dare not affirm anything beyond the reach of the eye, the sound of the ear, the touch of the finger-tips. But the beauties we see are only the reflections of the beauties that are, like Plato's artizans in the cave, catching only the reflected light from the realm above; the music we hear, the merest jingle of the melodies divine; the things we touch, the superficial, mechanical, material, side of reality. Why can't we believe that the unseen things which can be detected from the heights are those that are worth while, because the abiding, the eternal.

Only from the heights can we dominate bodily conditions. For there we dare affirm spiritual freedom, and sever the chains of appetite and passion, and deny the slavery of sense, and repudiate the bondage of matter, and bury negation and weakness and fear. In the depths, even upon the plane, bodily conditions dominate us, and like demons seeking to be housed, the imps of worry, melancholy, and despair rush in where angels fear to tread.

Sorry sphere that, to affirm that you are strong in the Lord. Deplorable place to develop energy, vitality, and power. Hopeless realm for the culture of love, light, harmony, and truth. O living soul, grope not thy way longer amid fog and night mist, with the whole horizon full of cloud and storm. Rise to the privilege of a child of

God. Breathe in the sunshine of the Father's face. Embody the infinite supplies of health from those high sources whence the full tides of the Spirit have their rise.

Once more, the mind of Christ will help you build a new-world order in which to live. What profit to gain the world and lose yourself? The soul is, indeed, a pilgrim and a stranger on the earth. Let it tent there for a night. But wo be to thee if there thou seek permanence and if thy holiest aspirations become dissipated therein.

On what things do you fasten your attention as you pass along? What pictures do you hang up in the mind's corridors? What delineation do you draw upon memory's walls? Each drawing executed by your thought and emotion is a life contribution to cheer or haunt you in the city of your hopes. You can not escape them, for they have character, substance, strength, and the more you gaze upon them the more like them you become. The old-world disorder is a poor resting-place for an immortal soul. The kingdom that comes down from heaven is the only safe place for God's children to dwell. That is the new-world order that endures. There all the soul needs for its completion is found. It is filled with light and inspiration, grace. and truth. Then, what pictures your thinking can paint, what sculptures your thought can chisel, what dreams of health and beauty you can weave, for you are giving expression of the God within you.

Ruskin caught the idea when he said: "Every right action and true thought sets the seal of its beauty on person and face." Even Confucius mirrored it when he said: "Exercise the mind with high contemplation and the body with gracious action, and so preserve the health of both." Epictetus saw it, tho as through a darkened glass, when he said: "Seek to converse in purity with your own pure mind and God. Purity of soul is best." John Milton affirmed it when he said: "A mind not to be changed by place or time; the mind is its own place, and in itself can make a heaven of hell, a hell of heaven." All are commentary on the Scriptures, which is man's guide from the plains to the heights, from the now to the by and by, from the old-world disorder to the unity and harmony divine, and which declared, centuries ago, "As a man thinketh in his heart, so he is." "Let this mind be in you which was also in Christ Jesus."

II

THE POWER OF THE SUBCON-
SCIOUS SELF

For the good that I would do, I do not, but the evil which I would not, that I do —New Testament Scriptures.

I am come that ye might have life, and that ye might have it more abundantly.—New Testament Scriptures

Every man has in himself a continent of undiscovered character.
Happy is he who acts as the Columbus of his own soul.
                                        —Sir J. Stephen.

One world is away and by far the largest to me and that is myself.
                                        —Walt Whitman.

II

THE POWER OF THE SUBCONSCIOUS SELF

Psychology's revelation of the mind's comprehensive realm
—Instances of the latest power of the subconscious—
Our new physician, Dr. V. M. N.—How Christianity
helps out—The nearness of the individual subconscious to the universal life—How men can block up or
open the health channels.

A THOUGHT is not only a fact, but a very serious fact. It has literal value in every possible and in all unforeseen ways. It is the most substantial thing with which our life has anything to do. There is no such thing as an idle thought. Every thought is an active, positive, influential something that creates commotion within the mind, good or ill, blessing or curse without. Few know of the tremendous power exerted by their thoughts. If we did, we would think them more carefully, express them more precisely, cultivate them more diligently, and use them more remedially. The within is always superior to the without. The one is the formative, the other the incidental. The external should be what the internal decrees. The circumstantial—what the personal ordains. It is a sad perversion of the divine order when environment dominates the man. All education, culture, religion, are that the person, the living soul, becomes strong enough to dominate his fate.

Viewpoint is everything. A gloomy mind means a gloomy world, however brightly the sun shines. A cheery mind fashions a cheery universe, tho the day be dark and dreary. A weak and troubled mind postulates an impossible resting-place. A strong mind demands a helpful rather than a hindering environment and empowers both hand and foot to sweep obstacles out of the way.

Dr. Matthews' helpful little book on ''How to Keep Well'' exclaims: ''There are mental as well as physical causes of disease to be considered. Your thoughts are of vast importance. A large proportion of all diseases are due directly or indirectly to thoughts. You think, then you act. An effect follows your act, which is good or bad. Thoughts are always first. Acts are always second. Effects are always third. Thoughts can produce disease as readily as germs. A man thinks he must have certain things to drink. He acts by taking them. He gets congestion of the membrane which lines the kidneys as an effect. In time the congestion reaches a state of inflammation, and then the kidney tissue breaks down and wastes away. This is kidney disease produced from thoughts. This illustration applies to a long list of diseases, as real and fatal as those produced by physical causes. Wrong thinking produces wrong acting, and wrong acting produces disease in a multitude of ways.''

Why not say, then, that the mental attitude we take toward everything determines its effects upon us?

But what is the self that is well or ill. Who can say? It is as mysterious as is God. The Bible exclaims, ''Great is the mystery of godliness.'' But it declares also that we are fearfully and wonderfully made. The majority of men make the self synonymous with the body. When we go home we will say to our friend, ''I was at church to-night.'' Perhaps we were. Or, we may have been a thousand miles away, visiting friends in a distant city, engaged in far-away occupations, or anticipating joys and sorrows we may never share tho a body called by our name, and that resembled us, sat in one of these pews. I thought I saw you here. But I saw only an intelligent-looking body. I must see your motives, your disposition, your loves and hates, your aspirations and longings and hopes before I can say I see you.

How tall are you? How much do you weigh? Six feet tall, you say, and weigh a hundred and fifty pounds? Both of us are wrong. You can't measure the self by a foot rule, nor weigh it in iron scales. Every time you aspire, and hope, and love you escape the body and live in the heights and distances. To estimate you aright I must gather up all your hopes and aspirations and faiths and loves; and if you have been wise enough to reach up and lay hold of the Eternal I must weigh and measure the Eternal in order to estimate you.

Others identify the self with the soul, but the problem is not simplified. The psychologist brings in mind to estimate aright. But how deepens the mystery, for the mind is no longer the man's consciousness only. Its seat is no longer in the brain alone. It inhabits the entire body and has other residence besides. All psychologic discovery includes in the term mind all possible mental states. Its domain is extended into all psychic action. It includes the conscious, and because consciousness is an infinitesimal part of its content it stretches forth unto all subconscious depths beside.

All vital experience is lodged in subconsciousness. The conscious experience is limited to the present. The sum total of experience stretching over the ranges of the years is safely stored away in subconsciousness, but not beyond recall. In fact, it is this reserve force on which we draw for guidance that constitutes the worth of life.- The real of our existence is never what we experience daily, hourly; it is rather the residue constantly filtering through consciousness into the depths of being, making us the men and women that we are. All the little and great events of life are stored away in subconsciousness beyond the reach of will, beyond the play of the desires, beyond the incidents and accidents of time. They are not influenced by consciousness, and will, and desire, but they constantly guide us, correct us, dominate us, lead us joyously in the paths of righteousness, else sorrowfully in the ways of sin.

How discouraging that we can not retain the whole of the book we read yesterday. By to-morrow nine-tenths of it has escaped us. Yes, escaped us, but only passed down into the subconscious part, as influence, to strengthen instinct, to prompt intuition, to form habit, to determine character.

So of our contact with the world or with truth. The passing conscious moment is trivial compared to what has passed through and down into reserve force to make strong for good or ill, to incite, prompt, decree, control, inspire, or impede.

We congratulate ourselves upon being reasonable beings, upon thinking before we speak, reflecting before we act, investigating before we affirm. But that's exactly what we do not do. The wisest part of life is lived by instinct. We reach conclusions by intuition:

we are ruled by habit. Character holds the helm and steers the ship. To say all this is to affirm that in the subconscious self resides the power, else we would have no power at all. Had a man only the cash he is conscious of in his pockets, he is weak indeed. It is his stored-away investments and the amount in the banks he can draw on in emergency that determine how rich he is.

Herein is the power of habit. Sometimes it carries us our way; sometimes its way. Much of the excuse we offer for evil doing is that habit led us there. We had no power of inhibition. The horse ran away, and we sat in the carriage helpless and let him run. When the horse is running our way, let him go. The faster the better! But we should always hold the reins, and so firmly that he is never allowed to take the bit in his teeth. Habit's way should be our way, else it should be pulled up with a round turn. That sounds like the recommending of sudden volitional action, an experiment that will not always work, especially when we want it to. Better to keep correcting habit in the forming, little by little, and then it will express the real and true self so accurately that our actions can be reckoned on in advance.

Conscious action is always weak action and hampered. Unconscious action is strong and free. If in leaving your home to-morrow for your work you say I will improve my walk, thus consciously place your feet this way and that, you will not walk at all. The walking that spells advancement and carries you along must be unconscious to be strong, sure and swift. Your unconscious life must direct you. Your instincts rather than your reason must force your steps.

The same with you, ladies, at the piano. Consciousness of notes and fingers kills the harmonies and prevents all freedom of action. Unconscious acting is the soul speaking through keys and notes and fingers guided by intuition, and regulated by habit.

We ministers know what a troublesome handicap consciousness is. One of the very simplest acts of his Sabbath ministrations is a witness. It is the repeating of that most simple, most beautiful, most familiar of all prayers, the Lord's Prayer. Many a minister will not repeat it. He is afraid to

do so. He fears he will not say it right.
Some have been known to write it out and
read it, lest to shut out the world with the
closed eyes is to shut out the precious words
as well. Clergymen have been known to repeat certain clauses of it, to leave out others,
to get twisted generally, and end in confusion, to the dismay of their worshipful congregations, who can't imagine what's up.
What is up? His sermon runs along
smoothly enough. His own prayer is consistent, accurate, logical, helpful. In the other
exercises he gives no evidence of paresis.
Only this is up. Through fear of saying
the Lord's Prayer wrongly he intrudes his
consciousness. He won't let it say itself. He
won't let subconsciousness caper. He is
so anxious to say it right that he says it
wrong.

But alas! In the subconsciousness is the
power of evil as well as the power of good.
The apostle gives us some startling auto-
biography just here. He would do the good,
but evil creeps up into consciousness and
holds him back. Instinctively his old dead
nature that he thought himself rid of, that

his Christianized reason abhors, obtrudes itself, and he finds conscious mind and volition, hands and feet, doing the very thing his reason condemns. Are we not all influenced as was he? Often it is the very height of our ideals, and in contrast the consciousness of a nature dominated by sense impressions and the lusts of the flesh that inspires the sad confession.

You never catch the Divine Master speaking thus. He is never conscious of unrealized ideals, of struggling from the depths to the heights, of striving to attain and of being thwarted in the pursuit. His consciousness and subconsciousness were always at one. There was no trail of the serpent in His life. Thus could He safely challenge His enemies to accuse Him if they dare of sin. "Who shall deliver me?" cries Paul. "Who accuseth Me?" cries Jesus. Christ's consciousness of God was so complete that it was perfect. Well may He be called the Perfect Man. Paul is with us on the plains. Jesus was with God on the heights. You may question the Virgin birth. You may ask the how and the where of the incarnation. But there He was, imperial, supreme. Account for Him who can. The consciousness of Jesus is the satisfactory solution of the problem that our dogmatism failed to reach.

Herein is the secret of his all-powerful influence that there seems to have been no break between His consciousness and His subconsciousness. That is why His influence has come down through all these centuries of time under the name of Christianity. We think of Christianity as a teaching of the Bible, as a moral code, as a bundle of heavenly precepts, or as a high and happy state of civilization. Why not call it what it is? Christ's influence coming down through the years. That unique unity between what He was conscious of possessing and what He actually had stored away in the subliminal depth of his life was the atonement behind whatever atonement He afterward achieved. There was no break between His conscious and His unconscious life. Paul felt the contrast. We are martyrs to the contradiction. Upon this matter of influence, as upon that of evil and good, we can exclaim, "The good I would I do not; the evil I would not that I do.''

We recognize the obligation to influence a person for good. It may be in the home among the children. It may be in our industrial or social life. So we begin a repression of ourselves all along the line. We weigh our words, count our acts, are careful of our thoughts. We pose, and are stilted and quite unnatural in that person's presence. And we wonder why he is not influenced when we've tried so hard. That's the trouble; we have tried so hard, and the harder we tried the weaker the influence. Conscious action is necessarily limited and weak. Self-consciousness is about the nearest thing to spiritual death that anywhere exists. Another reason for our failure is, doubtless, that the full force of our subconscious life was influencing the other way. Not only was our artificial self defeating our purpose, but our real self was defeating that purpose too. When shall we see that from the subconscious self all influence radiates, because there it is stored? Thus it is that in spite of us it is our unconscious influence that counts—the thing we do off guard. Our nature is always expressing itself. Influences steal out from it as do light-beams from the sun.

All such reflection is merely illustrative of the power of the subconscious. It dominates situations. It corrects ills. It goes far as a remedial agency in preventing and curing disease.

Dr. Schofield startles us by the statement that every doctor is in the presence of another and greater physician, "Dr. V. M. N.," a doctor trained in no human school, but divinely gifted to heal all varieties of disease and to repair every species of injury—the *vis medicatrix naturæ*—in other words, the unconscious mind.

"Every thoughtful practitioner," states Dr. Wilkinson, "will acknowledge that when his therapeutic reserves are exhausted, by far the most reliable consultant is the *vis medicatrix naturæ*. To ignore the fact that he has been in charge of the case for days, when we first approach with our mixtures and tabloids, is at least a mistake in medical ethics." In another place, Dr. Schofield exclaims,

[95]

"The truth is that nervous diseases require far more careful, well-devised, and elaborately carried-out treatment than any other ailment, because here Dr. V. M. N., himself is ill, and can not cooperate as in other diseases with the physician."

But the curative power of the subconscious is enhanced mightily by Christianity. Hear Dr. Matthews again state, in his recommendation of right thinking as necessary to right acts and results: "Christianity is the greatest teacher of right thinking, and its wonderful power to prevent disease is just beginning to be realized. That it is the greatest power in the world to prevent disease no doctor who has had practise and experience enough to know doubts. No one can realize better than a doctor what an amazingly large percentage of diseases result from immorality, dissipation, and weak will-power, from ignorance, from unclean thinking and unclean living—in short, from leading lives the Bible condemns on every page. Perhaps fifty per cent of all diseases is due directly or indirectly to these causes. Can Christianity prevent fifty per cent of the sickness that now prevails? I believe it can. But it must be directed to that end. Electricity is a great power. Applied one way it produces heat; in another way, light; in another it moves machinery; in another it transmits messages. So Christianity applied in one way civilizes and lifts up; in another way it purifies the heart; in another it prevents disease. There will be a great awakening throughout the world when people realize that Christianity prevents disease and adds years to human life. It pays to be a Christian right here in this world, without any reference to a future world.''

Now we are prepared to catch the strong, rich word of Christ: ''I am come that ye might have life and have it more abundantly.'' Back of all Christ's saving power is His unique ability as a revealer. He was the light of the world. He illumined the dark problems and cleared up the strange mysteries relating to God, eternity, man, and man's destiny. He showed our accessibility to the Infinite Power, the eternal life of God. He revealed eternal life's adaptability to us as a buoyant, uplifting divine force.

Even materialists recognize the presence of omnipotent power. Herbert Spencer asserts that ''we are in the presence of an Infinite Power which forms all things.'' Everything, even every atom of force in the universe, represents God's power. The stars shine by it. The flowers bloom by it. The tiny grass-blade grows by it. In nature it is a natural power, but no less divine. In mind it is a mental power, but no less divine. In the soul it is spiritual, there universally recognized as divine. It takes the name of the sphere and life to which we apply it.

Our finite life is a part of the Infinite. It is ever correcting, expanding, and lifting us above our limitations. As the author of ''Festus'' says:

We live in deeds, not words.
In thoughts, not breaths.
In feelings, not in figures on a dial.
We should count time by heart-throbs.
He most lives who thinks most, feels the noblest, acts the best.

Ralph Waldo Trine exclaims: ''In the degree that you realize your oneness with this Infinite Spirit of Life and thus actualize your latent possibilities and powers, you will exchange disease for ease, inharmony for harmony, suffering and pain for abounding health and strength. And in the degree you realize this wholeness, this abounding health and strength in yourself will you be able to carry it to all with whom you come in contact, for health is contagious as well as disease.''

The Eternal is the divine power in which time and all time's interests are set, as is the island in the sea; and if there be any little creeks and bays and inlets there, however far up into the interior of the land they reach, the cleansing, health-producing flow of the ocean runs up into those indentures, giving them beauty and usefulness. We are in the Church; are we any the less in Brooklyn? We live in the city; live we any less truly in the State, the nation, the world? So are we in the midst of time; are we any the less in the midst of the eternal? As Paul said: ''In Him we live and move and have our being.'' The eternal arms are underneath, not only holding us up, but the whole world besides. And oh! the joy of resting, not only upon the solid foundations of nature, but upon that which is more solid still, and making the foundations of nature strong enough to support.

Open then, friend, to the inflow of the Eternal. Don't dam up the channels. Bays and inlets human, as bays and inlets natural, become ill-smelling, miasmic, and an offense if we do.

Men block the channels through doubt, gloom, and despair. Men keep out the inflow through fear, worry, and anger. Men lose sight of the rising tide through reliance on the senses. The majority of men lose the blessings of health, rest, and ease through self-reliance, self-consciousness, and a positive tho unconscious determination not to let God in. But if all these human conditions shut out the inrush of the Eternal waters that bring cleansing, happiness, and life, thank God men can dig new channels of faith, hope, and love! And these are the most awarding endeavors, the most substantial and fruitful exertions man ever undertakes. Our curse is our reliance upon things, our identification with circumstances, our consciousness of self and self's poor ability.

Our blessing is in reliance upon the Eternal. And it is the subconscious self that is splendidly susceptible to the surrounding, near-by remedial power of God. That realm of the self not being under the rule and sway of the finite consciousness is in close touch with the invigorating purity of the Infinite Life. Let the precious God power in. Then is our natural effectiveness enhanced a hundredfold. If consciousness must assert itself that you know yourself to be a man, let it be encouraged in attachment to the Christ. Then it is that you willingly, cheerfully, unreservedly make connections with the abundant life of God. And all the precious depths of life become rich in spiritual reserve which buoys you up in emergency, makes the earth life a glad, sweet song and at the last floats the little boat of existence with its precious freight of experience, and with you, its lone but by no means lonely occupant, out of the inlet and bay across the bar, where Tennyson was to greet his pilot, into the harbor that is radiant with the nearer light of His face.

III

THE POWER OF SUGGESTION

*Jesus said, Get thee hence, Satan. . . . . Then the
devil leaveth him; and behold, angels came and ministered
to him.*—NEW TESTAMENT SCRIPTURES.

We may become gods, walking above the flesh.
—ATHANASIUS.

The soul is form and doth the body make.
—EDMUND SPENSER.

Build thee more stately mansions, O my soul!
As the swift seasons roll!
Leave thy low-vaulted past!
Let each new temple nobler than the last,
Shut thee from heaven with a dome more vast,
Till thou at length art free,
Leaving thine outgrown-shell by life's unresting sea.
—OLIVER WENDELL HOLMES.

III

THE POWER OF SUGGESTION

Evil and sickness, as well as all possible good and health in the subconscious—The curative value of suggestion—The part reason plays—Superstition—Deceptive health-resort cures—The power of suggestion in heredity, environment, advertisement, political and social leadership—The natural hypnosis of sleep—Curing your child of fears and evil habits — Pre-natal suggestion — The world's greatest battle-field one where suggestions are weapons.

IF good only were stowed away in the depths of the subconscious self, all would be well; our instincts would be true, our intuitions unerring, our habits correct, our entire life abounding in health and blessing. But, alas, evil is stored there, too, and consciousness of weakness and thoughts of sickness and pictures of obstacles and of all conceivable ills. The old-world disorder has wrought havoc with us. It caught us on its own plane and holds us prisoner, pounding us with blows, vexing us with friction, depressing us with gloom, beguiling us with deceits, and binding us with entanglements.

We had no right to be there tampering with forbidden things. But we wanted experience and we got it—got it bad. We craved the fruit of all the trees save the tree of life, and they turned to apples of Sodom in our clutch. We touched and tasted and handled the pleasing things along all the avenues of sense-gratification, and received sorrow for our pains and dissatisfaction for our reward.

What shall be the remedy for the abounding evil and the spreading sickness there? Thank God, there is a remedy at our hand, so simple, so strong, so rich that its curative force is difficult to realize and incredible to believe. It is the power of suggestion. How vague and unsubstantial the term sounds. But it is one of the most potent forces, so exclaims the psychologist, in existence. It will pull down evil and build up good within the soul more speedily and surely than all the remedial punishments of earth. It will transform character more effectively than could the thundering of Sinai. It will change the course of fate more suddenly and violently than could all the shocks of doom.

Yes, it is mysterious and subtle, but very powerful withal, even tho it is only a hint to the soul as a stimulant, an incentive to action.

Poor soul, cramped, crowded, supprest, impoverished, sick. It needs all the encouragement it can get. Beside the evil instincts, wrong habits, sickening realizations that have sprouted there and drawn their nourishment from its precious soil, are now implanted rich, strong, pure thoughts, righteous tendencies, inducements to health, encouragements to victory. And the mysterious thing about it all is that these will take root there when patiently and persistently introduced, and will spring up and choke out the weeds.

Whether or not the remedial suggestions are successful depends upon whether we can get them into the life. Reason is always there on guard. It is given us by God to guard the life from outside interference. It both keeps our emotions from running away with us and holds outside inducements in check. An external force must show itself reasonable to be admitted. All new ideas,

all strange suggestions, must be in keeping
with reason's preconceived beliefs of right
and good. In short, reason must be respected. The only alternative is to ignore it
and demand that its hold upon the citadel
be weakened. This is achieved if the person
needing the help trusts the one offering the
suggestion. If not, reason must be beguiled,
and self-consciousness side-tracked.

Such is achieved through hypnosis.
There we have uttered the word that
awakens criticism because so poorly understood. Its remedy is purely negative. It
simply prepares the conditions for what follows. It cures not. It only removes restrictions. It makes the man irrational and
unconscious, and relaxed and receptive
enough for the putting into the deep-reaching
inward parts the needed suggestion. But
of the few difficult cases I have been instrumental in helping through the introduction
of these remedial principles, I have not seen
one where hypnosis was needed had I the
ability or desire to wield so powerful a force.
Distrest souls are only too glad to will reason
to step aside, that the curative suggestion

may come in. They relax cheerfully. Self-consciousness is laid by for the time being. The subconscious depths are presumably laid bare to receive the invigorating thoughts. Natural sleep, however, is one of the most promising conditions for the introduction of suggestion.

So far we have spoken as tho suggestion were a rare force, and employed always remedially, and by the trained dispenser of health and good cheer. But the fact of the matter is that it is the most present, commonplace truth in existence. Everything that exists of any influence generates suggestion. Look at the mysteries by which we are surrounded. Whatever the mind can not comprehend and attribute intelligible cause to exerts more suggestive force than the understood. The incomprehensible is a potent suggestive force over the average mind. We are all more or less sensitive to the mysterious. Imagination is aroused, fancy stirred, credulity stimulated: Cartright truly exclaims:

Fancy can save or kill; it hath closed up
Wounds when the balsam could not, and without
The aid of salves—to think hath been a cure.

[109]

The understood, the solved, soon lose interest for us. The charm of life is in the new of life. Distance lends enchantment. Familiarity breeds contempt. Conceal your limitations from the vulgar throng if you would hold their respect. Reveal them only to those who love you. They only can be trusted not to throw you down. It is because the world's plumb-lines are not long enough to sound your depths that you have any influence over the world. So, too, has the world's mystery influence over its curious, questioning children. The so-called worldly man is he whom the world has filled to the brim with suggestions. Its mystery awakens his curiosity and fascinates his soul, as do painted circus clowns make children laugh.

Think of the superstitions the power of mystery awakens. In Egypt, flies by the scores and hundreds feast on the children's faces that are never washed, as do the dogs upon the refuse in the streets of Constantinople, which are never cleaned. These flies are allowed to eat out the children's eyes, inducing sores and blindness, because of superstition that if they were brushed away the child would die. Why single out Egypt? Every country has many superstitions for its stock in trade. Every civilization, as well as every religion, holds its devotees through manifold customs and sanctions and traditions that are grounded in mystery, and through which the light of reason never shines. Lessing says we are swayed by our superstitions even after we understand them.

Now, it is this superstition that an age-long suggestion produces, that accounts for innumerable cures at certain world centers, such as Lourdes, with its shrines, and altars, and charms, and numerous bones of saints, where ailing pilgrims leave a million and a half dollars every year. And what of cures by relics and idols in India, China, Africa, and in the cases of multitudes who touch the holy coat of Treves? And there are you, carrying a chestnut in your pocket or wearing a metal ring on a certain finger to ward off rheumatism. Have they virtue? Yes, just as much as your belief endows them with.

And there are the devotees at the numerous continental spas, with their invigorating mineral waters and sulfur, soda, iron, and mud baths. Do the physicians in attendance at these fashionable centers really believe in the efficacy of these material agencies, or is the therapeutic power largely one of suggestion to the latent resourcefulness of the subconscious mind? All these mysterious symbols exert a tremendous suggestive power which the soul, crying dumbly for relief from its thraldom, accepts. And the moment the mind sees health in the ideal, that the priest or the charlatan assures the confiding soul is guaranteed by the charm, that moment the mind begins to create health in the real. To picture health mentally is to create health mentally. And what the mind creates will be surely and immediately exprest throughout the body. At first so faintly as to be unrealized, but afterward remedially, through persistence of application to the body's needs.

Then there is the suggestive force of heredity. We all carry much of that with us. We can trace back certain tendencies to father or mother, certain characteristics back further still for generations into the dim past. Many make this force of heredity responsible for the possession of bad habits, which consciousness of possession seems to paralyze all endeavors for reform. There is much erroneous thinking about this thing. Evil habits are not transmitted. No heredity has as much power actually as have we potentially. No man need remain for two consecutive hours in the clutch of moral heredity anyway. Only a weakened nerve condition is handed down, which condition can readily be overcome by strong suggestions and self-control.

Then what about the constant stream of suggestions from environment, ever flowing into and leaving their impressions upon the conscious and subconscious states? Everything surrounding us exerts influence here. We constantly take on the influences of the situation by which we find ourselves surrounded. Is the sea voyage stormy, how upset we also are! Is the ocean calm, how rested are we in consequence! Is the weather continuously disagreeable, we find it hard to keep our equilibrium; while sunny skies and balmy south breezes make serene the soul.

A few years ago in a certain part of England the weather was so continuously beastly —that's the term they used—that at last, wearying of looking at the barometers day after day, week in and week out, the entire inhabitants of a certain seaport town, in sheer disgust, gathered up their weather-glasses and dumped them into the old junk-shops. Both the weather and the barometers flooded the people with disagreeable suggestions. They could not do away with the weather, but they could with their barometers, that seemed to serve no better purpose than to accentuate their discontent.

Just here is felt the force of advertisement. Any patent medicine, however worthless, will make its advocate rich if he will only persist in advertising it. The dear public succumb in the long run. They can not stand up under the continuous force of his big-lettered suggestions. They rather enjoy being humbugged. What splendid advantage the big stores take of this weakness on our part! All they need do is to keep offering suggestions of cheapness, or of the supposed worth and imagined usefulness of their wares, and multitudinous innocent ones, whose sole interests the advertiser seems to have at heart, take hold of the tempting bait.

Political and social leaders take advantage of their constituencies with large success just here. It is a relentless power of suggestion that they wield over their thoughtless followers. The term "boss" for the political leader is well coined. He plies his vocation relentlessly. He works his clientage to the limit.

The important consideration is, shall we take worthy advantage of this natural tendency by supplying the highest, truest, mental, moral, spiritual suggestion to supply the need? It is no small responsibility that the guardians of your life assume, the physician, whether of the body or of the soul; the father and mother in the home; the teacher in the school; the nurse in the hospital; all who influence weaker souls; all whose position it is to minister either preventively or remedially to the afflicted.

We said a while ago that the state of natural sleep was the most receptive time for sending suggestions into the child's life, or into the depths of an adult life, for that matter, whom you would help. Is your little one afraid of the dark, as so many little ones are? Sit by his bedside for a few nights, and say to him with low, strong, hopeful, assuring word: "Do not fear the dark, my boy. There is nothing to harm you. God has given it to you to rest in, so that you will be strong and fresh for your work and play on the morrow. The darkness is your friend, not your enemy. Be a brave and heroic little man in the darkness as well as in the light."

Is your boy or girl forming bad habits? Threat and punishment often awaken resentment and strengthen the very self-consciousness you should try to dethrone and get under and behind. How much easier, during sleep, calmly, lovingly to talk and think heroic remedies into the precious life! Is the tendency of the life toward intemperance, immorality, or some bad habit that will degrade his manhood and ruin all your hopes? Give strong hints to the wide-awake self behind the sleeping self—the self that is never more alert and interested and receptive than now that the check of self-consciousness is lifted. There you have a condition of natural hypnosis that invites your healthy ideals, your moral convictions, your optimistic thought in that life's behalf. In your thought and speech identify him with his latent manhood, his strongest self; remind him that the self he manifests each day is only his diseased and superficial self, and that your sympathetic help and all infinite power are helping him to victory.

Remember the mind begins to create in the actual what it sees in the ideal, and what it sees in the ideal is what you impart to it. You are invigorating the soul for action, and the sphere of that activity will be the body in which that soul resides. The soul is a good housekeeper. Its desire is always to keep the little tenement of its residence well furnished and in order. But the servant problem presses here as in other spheres. It needs to be given reliable information, the best courage, the strongest faith, the truest ideals, and assurances of victory. With such loyal waiting maids as these, the soul will press forward unto all splendid achievement and righteousness.

But what about the type of motherhood and fatherhood needed for the task? The flippant, dissipated, superficial rearer and governor of children will not suffice. It is not the words spoken into the listening stillness of the child's life that solves the problem. It is the affectionate heart-throb and soul-potency that count. It is the pure, true thought that is effective. It is the deepest mother-love that is the suggested force.

Then, perhaps, more important still is that pre-natal power of influence that makes for good or ill, mental and moral strength or weakness, in proportion as the invisible mother-world holds not only a developing little life, but the most important God-given opportunity to mold that precious angel charge as she may. Here is the most fruitful and satisfactory source of mental, moral, and religious suggestion she will ever be able to embrace. Now it is that she needs a nearby world of high, rich, true thoughts and emotions to draw on. She has it in her power to make that little life, while yet distinctly in her own sweet keeping, just the kind of a boy or girl in temperament, in mental endowment, in moral significance, that she may choose.

We spoke incidentally of the trained nurse, so called, and her helpful hospital work. But, believe me, the day is not far off when to be a "trained" nurse she, as well as the physician that directs her, must know much of the psychic treatment of bodily ills. She can save life in an emergency by the power of health suggestions, even after her best manual skill fails. She can put new determination into the flagging will, new courage into the weakening heart, new strength into the wavering spirit that if not called back to its responsibilities may slip away, unto a healthier, more spiritual body that it have more perfect medium of expression. We all know that good nursing is the indispensable something in sickness. But good nursing to be most efficient should work upon the sick one's mind as truly as upon his body.

Our meditation upon the power of suggestion can not be complete without mention of

the greatest source of powerful suggestion
in existence—the greatest, the most powerful because divine. It is the Bible. What
a storehouse of the best suggestion! Its precepts stored away in the soul's depths become our truest safeguard against that mental and moral derangement that is ever
expressing itself in bodily ills innumerable.
And what is the Christianity of which we are
all proud, and which the Bible so forcibly defines, but a stream of life-giving, divine suggestion making us strong and righteous,
amidst the sinful tendencies and the evil
suggestions of the years?

The temptation of Jesus in the wilderness reveals a battle-ground of contend-
ing forces along this line, and in the
terms of our thinking. There they are,
the entire world possibilities of evil on
the one side, and the entire world possibilities of good on the other. And they fight
back and forth until one or the other is van-
quished. Talk of battle-fields! Waterloo,
when Wellington was victorious and Napoleon bit the dust, was momentous. And so
were Austerlitz and Gettysburg, but insig-

nificant compared to the wilderness of Judea. That was the world's most famous battle-field, for there the world's most significant battle was fought. And weapons more subtle and powerful than rifles, bayonets, and Gatling guns held sway. They were the weapons of suggestion, weapons of intense thought and spirit power.

From the world forces of evil comes the thrust of suggestion, "If thou be the Son of God command that these stones be made bread." And then from that divine embodiment of all good comes that counter-suggestion which parries the thrust, "It is written man shall not live by bread alone, but by every word that proceedeth out of the mouth of God."

Baffled but still alert the challenge rings out from the pinnacle of the temple: "Cast thyself down. His angels will hold thee up in their hands." But again the answer comes, "It is written that thou shalt not tempt the Lord thy God." Then is hurled forth a third suggestion, "All the kingdoms of the world for a moment's worship." And here repelled again, overborne and put completely to rout,

Satan retires from the conflict. And we read that God's angels come and minister with all heavenly suggestions unto Him, suggestions of strength, of joy, of a Father's satisfaction in a conquering Son, of opening heavens, of the "well done" of God.

Had evil that day conquered good, there would have been, so far as human eye can detect, no Christianity for the world, no Savior of men, no

> Strong Son of God. Immortal love
> Whom we that have not seen thy face,
> By faith, and faith alone, embrace,
> Believing where we can not prove.

Indeed the wilderness of Judea becomes the world's most momentous battle-field. Indeed, the weapons were the most powerful and dangerous that could be used. Indeed, Jesus is worthy of all honor as Master and Lord.

Notice that Christ's weapon of conquest was the word of God. Three distinct times He unsheathes the sword of the Spirit and wields it to the death. It is written. It is written. It is written. That is the all-conquering suggestion that never fails. Take it into your heart, friend, that you may be strong. Let verses, paragraphs, chapters of such divine resourcefulness filter down into your subconscious self and take root there, and fill up as with good seed all the precious soil. You then will fight your battle with evil gallantly, and lead your environment captive and dominate the world.

IV

THE POWER OF AUTOSUGGES-
TION

Ye shall know the truth and the truth shall make you free.—New Testament Scriptures.

Lord increase our faith.—New Testament Scriptures.

Make less thy body hence, and more thy grace.
—Shakespeare.

He was uglier than he had any business to be.
—Bulwer Lytton.

The acrid humors breaking out all over the surface of man's life are only to be subdued by a gradual sweetening of the inward spirit.
—Henry Drummond.

Let us fold away our fears,
And put by our foolish tears,
And through all the coming years
Just be glad.
—James Whitcomb Riley.

IV

THE POWER OF AUTOSUGGESTION

Its meaning—Inductive and deductive reasoning—Hudson's three statements—Autosuggestion in a hospital—Calling dying people back to health—The subconscious our faithful slave—How to apply autosuggestion—Three important cures—Christian Science's denial of nature and disease—Its cures all wrought by suggestion—The principles and responsibilities of motherhood.

THOSE are the ideal conditions; the truth, the enjoyment of its freedom, and the increase of our faith. Best of all, they can become realizations to every child of God in all the world, producing health, joy, and abundance of good cheer. The trouble is, we only half live. Doubt has closed the chambers of the soul. Error has shut to the blinds. The sunlight of God's face can't stream in through the windows, and the life is conscious only of restrictions; the limitations of nature, the crampings of environment, the permissions of reason, the hampering tendencies of the world. But blest realization when the soul sees that all these trammeling influences are lifeless conditions except when we endow them with vitality; and that the eternal life of God is pressing us from within and from without, ready to impart its richness and enlargement the moment we express faith in His ability to bless. Goethe has given us the secret to all this precious realization when he exclaims:

Are you in earnest? Seize this very minute;
What you can do, or dream, you can begin it.
Boldness has genius, power, and magic in it.
Only engage, and then the mind grows heated;
Begin, and then the work will be completed.

Exactly that is the encouragement psychology gives. Its revelations are amazing. It shows the realm of mind to be limitless; its conscious and subconscious powers measureless. Hudson makes three statements that are the basis of all remedial realization within the reach of every one; "that the subjective, or subconscious, mind is constantly susceptible to control by suggestion; that it is incapable of inductive reasoning; and that it has control of all the functions, conditions, and sensations of the body."

This fact makes the man the absolute controller of his fate. His life can become exactly what he chooses. He can make it a dungeon filled with gloom, and the cells of the brain will generate that gloom, and send it coursing down through all the cells of the body in all possible realizations of sickness. Or he can make the life a palace beautiful, wherein health abounds, and the realizations of truth abide.

This latter-day psychology forces upon us grave responsibility. All the processes of the subjective mind are deductive. You impart the premise from which its constructive work begins. You indicate the way it shall proceed. You awaken its instincts that exercise themselves swiftly and unerringly to conclusions that will bless or curse the life that God hath placed in its keeping.

What, then, shall be its content? You can have it what you will. Impart to this residential realm absurd ideas and false reasonings, and you are laying up accumulations of misery that will later express themselves in hideous forms to haunt your peace. But give it the enlightenment of truth; stimulate it with the assurances of faith; invite the angels of joy and hope to be its guests, then will the precious residue be healthful, and all its creative powers remedial of the body's ills.

Man is then his own educator, his own moral and religious teacher, his own physician. In no other sense than through the knowledge of the subtle relationship between the objective and subjective minds is it true that we are self-made men. The transmission of information by the objective mind to the subjective is what the psychologist calls autosuggestion. It can negative all heterosuggestion, coming from heredity, environment, and external minds, and becomes the soul's most reliable source of information.

A soldier volunteer in the recent Spanish-American war lay sick with typhoid fever in a Southern hospital. The physician passing through the ward on his tour of inspection noticed his weakened condition and said to the nurse in attendance, ''That man can't live.'' The young man overheard the remark, and with what remaining strength he had cried out, ''I will live!'' The physician's remark aroused his antagonism and impelled an autosuggestion contradictory to the physician's declaration. The determination to live started all the curative forces of his subconscious nature, and the ideal of life, "I will live!" crowded out the expectations of death. He did live.

At no time is suggestion so powerful for life or death as when the patient is on this mysterious borderland. Even when the person is unconscious or delirious, the exprest suggestion of life or death on the part of an attendant falls not on deafened ears. The sicker the man, and the less conscious he is, the more awake and alert is the subconscious self. Then it is that the way is most open to suggestion. Then it is that the depths in which the curative power resides catch the convincing thought, and use it, sometimes with remarkable results.

Remember that it is the faith, hope and courage of the subjective mind that are needed for all therapeutic purposes, for it is that mind which controls the functions and conditions of the body. Give to it, then, suggestions of health. Remind it of its reserve power. Impart encouragements of conquest.

Inspire it with assurances of victory. Then order it to generate health and achieve life. You will be amazed at the willing service it will render, right along the line of your desire. It is glad to be your servant and recognize your right to command. Moreover, it awaits your initiative. That once given, it, strong in the confidence you have imparted, hastens with all speed to carry out your orders and achieve results.

You will see the reasonableness of all this when you realize that you, as a conscious, reasoning mind, are steering the life-craft. If, as many an unwise navigator before you has done, you allow yourself to become the creature of circumstances and lose your reckoning, your craft drifts into the shoals, and your companion in misery can not rectify your errors. If you are hopeless and afraid, because the fogs have shut out the light, your assistant can not find the harbor for you and guide you to safety. He is no navigator. He has no seamanship. He neither throws the lead for soundings, nor scans the compass and the weather-glass. His place is down below, keeping the fires going, keeping up the steam, and listening for your signals, that he may know your desire and act accordingly. You are the responsible one. You must keep the ship, with its valuable cargo of life issues and experiences and healthful realizations, off the rocks. But, under your guidance and at your command, with what alacrity and endurance will he struggle to save the ship! Let such illustration convince us of the relation between the objective, the conscious, and the subjective, the subconscious, minds.

Sleep, therefore, is the most favorable condition for the giving of commands and the imparting of encouragement to the subconscious life that you would correct of evil habit, or make well when sick; for in this state of natural hypnosis the control of the conscious, commanding mind of the recipient is relaxed, and you become the suggester, whose wishes and authority are to be carried out.

Such a quiescent condition is also admirable if it be self-suggestion that be contemplated. I mean that quiescent state just preceding sleep. We all have ideals for ourselves. In those ideals are pictured the kind of men and women we desire to be. Is there some evil habit holding you in thraldom? Think it all out, the kind of a person you would become. Project that thought into your deeper self, which is shortly to be entrusted with the watch-care of your destiny, when you yield up your consciousness in slumber; and just thinking desirously is the necessary projection. You will find in the morning that progress has been made toward the goal. Repeat the experiment each night, and each new day will bring reward.

Are you ill? Has the wear and tear of living got hold of your nerves? Has nervousness in some one of its multitudinous forms taken possession? Send thoughts of rest and health into the deeper realm of being. Your subconscious self will gladly receive them and bring its calm, strong resourcefulness into play in keeping with the hint, the indication that you give. That is autosuggestion. You have planted good seed in the soul. The remedial results will be wonderful to contemplate. All you need for belief in the reality of these healthful realizations is our present psychological knowledge that the subconscious mind is susceptible to control by suggestion, especially autosuggestion. Its power over the functions and conditions of the body is the sufficient reason for believing it to be true.

Let me emphasize persistence along this line. The value of frequent reiteration of a suggestion can not easily be estimated. Remember, you are dealing spiritually rather than intellectually with yourself. Frequent repetition of a word, a sentence, a thought is veriest intellectual nonsense, but both wise and consistent spiritually. Take such a clause as this, "I am free," or as this, "I am God's child," or, again, "I shall sleep to-night"; they have no intellectual attractiveness beyond the first mention of them, inasmuch as the intellect is ever looking for new words and meanings. But to the subconscious, the soul nature, such a simple definite sentence, if it contain what we are desirous of realizing, is the welcomed sign-post pointing to health, ease, and contentment. Frequent repeatings of some such simple, strong sentence is what makes the impression upon the life-depths. It is all forced endeavor at first, and for a considerable time perchance.

But after a while the oft-repeated suggestion lodged in those precious depths becomes not only an automatic force in subconsciousness, but in consciousness too. Then the remedial work is achieved. Then you rejoice in realization of the thing you need, for this reiteration of a suggestion means the development of any subjective activity that may be desired.

A further advantage should be noted here. Write out or print in large letters upon a spacious card the ideal you want actualized in your life. Place it upon the wall of your silence chamber, or in some convenient place where you can sit, or lie in most easeful and relaxed position with the eye fixt upon it. Do not merely gaze upon the motto. Yield yourself up to it completely. Close the eyes, to shut out everything, that the thought embodied in that little sentence may suffuse your entire being. Even a half-hour each day is not too long for such communion. After a few days of such meditation, the suggestion becomes an ever-present thought-companion. The busy hours of the day will not obliterate it. The wakeful, otherwise depressing hours of the night will be cheerfully endured.

I have in mind many instances of remedy resulting from this kind of health treatment.

I recall one whose life had been for years the prey of morbid fears, fears of sickness, of impending disaster, of losing friendships, of constant, irrational, indefinable happenings, who was cured thereof through the repeated contemplation of the large-lettered printed suggestion: "I have no fear. I am strong in the Lord."

I know of another person who had been for long the slave of passions, easily moved by lustful thought, readily swayed by sexual temptations, who was amazingly strengthened against them, even to a profest emancipation from their control, through a week's daily contemplation of this strong motto: "I am God's child. I am pure. The Spirit shall rule me." Such affirmation means the denial of the animal selfhood, and brings the submerged spirit of the afflicted one up and into a spiritual realm, where amidst feasting on spiritual suggestion, and the inbreathing of a spiritual atmosphere the self finds precious substitute for the old carnal realizations.

I recall a third person afflicted with awful insomnia who was cured through persistent contemplation of the printed suggestion, "I shall sleep to-night." This contemplation was, however, accompanied with the instruction not to try consciously to sleep, but after ten minutes' meditation each afternoon, and again each evening, to retire for the night absolutely indifferent as to whether he would sleep or not. This passage of Scripture was, however, recommended, "I will meditate on Thee in the night-watches." He was urged to change his attitude toward his insomnia. He was commanded to regard it as an opportunity of conscious quiet in which body and mind were being rested; moreover, to regard it an occasion for sweetest thoughts of God's presence.

Now what was the result? His very first night was spent in quietness rather than in feverish tossings and turnings, while his statement was, "I almost enjoyed my wakefulness; it was, at any rate, bearable for the first time in months." His second night's experience showed the period of sleep doubled in duration. Within a week or ten days he was enjoying a normal night's slumber. Better still, he was enjoying God's rest-restoring presence both by night and day.

Repetition will establish faith in a thing without the presentation of real facts to the person's mind. In fact, how many of our ideas have no scientific basis! There is no careful rational grounds for them whatsoever. Yet there they are. They came to us from our surroundings, our traditional training, even from our own or another person's superstitions, but what a powerful influence they exert upon our life!

Christian Science is a most emphatic illustration of this. Irrationality is rampant there; scientific confusion supreme. What of it if they are so long as the power of suggestion holds sway? Notice the content of that suggestion. Denial of disease. Denial of nature. Denial of the integrity of mortal mind. But in spite of its bad psychology and its erroneous mentality, it cures. The power of suggestion is the solution. The afflicted soul gives up its reasoning faculty, and surrenders all its preconceived opinions, and convictions for its life's sake, and taking in the practi-

[139]

tioner's irrational suggestions, acts upon them. "You are not sick. You have no pain.". "But," exclaims the afflicted one, "I am sick. I am conscious of the pain." "You are not sick," reiterates the healer. "You only think you are. Stop thinking so. Cease encouraging the errors of mortal mind." The afflicted one obeys. The subconscious self catches the persistent suggestion. For experiment's sake, the person denies the reality of the disease and pain. The suggestion of the practitioner becomes autosuggestion. The patient thus becomes his own physician, and a cure results. Whether or not this is so depends upon whether or not the afflicted one cooperates with the denial of his ills. Where cures are not effected is where a strong mentality can not deny that sensation of pain of which it is conscious.

Such a one visited me last week, herself both patient and practitioner, with the statement that she, with a score of her Christian Science friends, was attending these services and learning of the psychology of the very treatment they were practising, yet which none of them before had understood.

The best of it is, however, that such irrational denial is not necessary for a moment. Christian Science has stumbled upon a great health-producing principle with no more idea than the man in the moon how it got there. Nor does it know what it possesses, so far as its psychological content is concerned. Nor does it care. Fortunately, it does not have to. The law of suggestion operates so quickly, and mightily, and successfully, and always in spite of scientific precision, and the demands of reason, or even its presence, that Christian Science claims, and justly, the restoration of health; and the subconscious self, which cares no more for reason and science than does Christian Science itself, obeys the suggestion, does the necessary thing, and restores the harmony of the deranged life.

Let me repeat, however, that such denial of sickness and pain of nature, as well as of the skilled physician's aid; of scientific precision, and reason's logical processes are not necessary to effect curative results. God's healing ministry is ever at our door to be drawn on *ad infinitum* whenever we will. Denial of facts achieves nothing, save that it is a short-cut method to the very dethronement of the reason that all remedial suggestion needs to be operative. It must always be slid into the life surreptitiously. Its very nature demands that reason be caught off guard; thus sleep, or hypnosis, or volitional relaxation to get itself in past reason's police control. In the last analysis and so far as results go, what matter, then, whether reason be denied, or acknowledged and beguiled from its post of duty, else thrown out bodily as for the time being detrimental to the life's best interests?

But it is the solemn responsibility that I want especially to impress, for each life to guard its deposits, and safeguard its investments, and store away wisely in the safe-deposit vaults of the subconscious self. We all exert an influence upon one another and ourselves so far-reaching that only eternity will be able to reveal its full power.

We have said that the creative powers of the subconscious mind are measureless. They have no limit, yet discovered, save one; namely, the stimulus which spurs it to activity. Here we come upon distinctively religious

ground, for faith is that stimulus. Christian
faith is the subjective mind's strongest reliance. A weak and faltering faith diminishes
its activity in all remedial directions. Increase your faith, and its activity has become
accelerated marvelously. Faith that you are
God's child, faith in Christ's saving truth,
faith in your Heavenly Father's interest in
your welfare are equipment for which there
is no equivalent in all the universe. Such is
dynamic power that removes restrictions, lifts
existence from the earth-plane to spiritual
heights, and accomplishes realizations of enlargement that empower the soul for conquest
in all realms of experience. To be a Christian is God's greatest demand and life's supreme requirement.

I would say here in detail what I touched
upon in the preceding chapter concerning pre-
natal influence. Would that every maiden in
the land might read it. We often hear it
said that there are more women than men in
our churches. The same is, I presume, true
of the kingdom. Sad day, indeed, when it
ceases to be true for both, for therein is
the saving hope for both. It is shocking

perversion of a God-given order when womankind prefers the frivolity of the world to the sobering graces of religion. Manhood stands for strength and reason; but womanhood for enthusiasm and emotion, which, if reenforced by Christianity, conquers the world. You young ladies, through your influence in the homes of the nation as wives and mothers, are the most potent factors in the world's civilization. Are you being prepared for these responsibilities which in the providence of God will come to you sooner or later? The sphere of your grandest usefulness will be in the training of the young. When the All-Father puts a little new life into your keeping He has crowned you with His choicest blessing, for they tell me that the joys of motherhood are the world's divinest delights. In that glad day will you have a wealth of mental, moral, and spiritual suggestion to impart? Mother's thought and precept go farther, and sink deeper, than father's example and command. And before that little life emerges into the glad, sad world of things, while yet it is all your precious own, before its attention is shared by many another's influence and care, do you feel competent to impart to its tiny developing life those sweet graces of the true, the beautiful, the good? It will be that child's right to have the best God-sanctioned heritage in existence. But it can have no heritage that you yourself do not possess. It can dwell in no paradise that you do not inhabit. Let not its angel lineaments be overmarked with motherly frivolity and indifference. Let not its divine life be seared through the influence of a constitutionally weak, mentally depraved, morally corrupt womanhood that thinks of child-bearing as accident, and child-nurture as a perversion and restriction of freedom. Every individual is witness to the vitalizing power of love. But in all the universe of mortals no being is so susceptible to Christian motherly affection as the unborn child of her care.

Why not realize, all of us, the responsibility to live in a thought-world of sunshine, purity, and love? And if you carry about with you the conviction that God is lifting upon you the light of His face, that light will be deflected nowhere save into your mortal mind, producing cheer and purity and all the sweet graces of the Spirit. We shall realize sooner or later that every thought the mind entertains passes into influence of some kind upon the body. And every living cell throughout the entire human frame responds in sickness or in health, in blessing or in curse, to the impression the mind imparts.

Let there be many windows in your soul,
That all the glory of the universe
May beautify it. Not the narrow pane
Of one poor creed can catch the radiant rays
That shine from countless sources. Tear away
The blinds of superstition; let the light
Pour through fair windows, broad as truth itself
And high as heaven. Tune your ear
To all the wordless music of the stars
And to the voice of nature, and your heart
Shall turn to truth and goodness as the plant
Turns to the sun. A thousand unseen hands
Reach down to help you to their peace-crowned heights,
And all the forces of the firmament
Shall fortify your strength. Be not afraid
To thrust aside half truths and grasp the whole.

V

THE ALL-POWER OF THE UNI-VERSAL LIFE

In the day that God created man, in the likeness of God created He him.—OLD TESTAMENT SCRIPTURES.

God is spirit and they that worship Him must worship Him in spirit and in truth.—NEW TESTAMENT SCRIPTURES.

O God, I think thy thoughts after thee.
　　　　　　　　　　—JOHANN KEPLER.

So nigh the great warm heart of God, you almost seem to hear it beat.
　　　　　　　　　　—JAMES RUSSELL LOWELL.

Give me, O God, to sing this thought,
Belief in plan of Thee enclosed in Time and Space,
Health, Peace, Salvation, Universal,
Is it a dream?
Nay, but the lack of it the dream,
And failing it, life's love and wealth a dream,
And all the world a dream.
　　　　　　　　　　—WALT WHITMAN.

V

THE ALL-POWER OF THE UNI-VERSAL LIFE

Whence comes the curative force of the subconscious?—The universal mind in nature and the individual man—Man in God's image, and God in man's—The perfect unity between the conscious and subconscious natures of Jesus—Need of a new theology of a Christological nature—Man both chaos and cosmos—Remedial Christianity in Christian Science—New Thought upon the stage without as well as within the Church.

WE have said a good deal lately about the objective and subjective minds characteristic of the individual, also of the relations between them. The one you remember is that which reasons inductively, investigates, differen-tiates, selects, classifies. The other cares nothing for these exercises, but works deduct-ively. It receives whatever thought you give, as well as all impressions coming from its environment, its heredity, its own or other minds, and works swiftly and accurately to the conclusion in keeping with the sugges-tion. Add to this knowledge that other, of its creative and recreative control of all bodily

[149]

functions and conditions, and you will realize the tremendous possibilities within our keeping.

But what is this curative force of the individual subjective mind? What the nature of this mysterious realm? What the character of this soil which holds such latent richness that it sprouts quickly good seed, truth thoughts, health tendencies, when such are imparted to its care? The secret of it all is this: that it is the same subjective mind which is at work throughout the universe, expressing itself in nature everywhere, imparting life to its multitudinous forms, the flower of the field, "the primrose by the river's brink," the budding trees, the springing grass, the rolling sea-waves, the bounding river, the falling rain, the shining stars, the existence of animal and vegetable, and all conceivable natural forms. It gives life to ourselves also, enabling the eye to see, the ear to hear, the heart to beat, the mind to think, all the functions of the body to abide in health and do their work; all the phenomena of the universe to be manifest in strength and beauty and truth. The universal mind is the creative force throughout nature, ever gathering up the waste materials that nothing be lost, revitalizing, reorganizing, constantly making all things new. Wherever we find creative power at work we are in the presence of the power of the universal subjective mind, whether it be working on the large scale in the cosmos or in the miniature realm of the individual.

Aristotle said the state is the man writ large. Plato said nature is the macrocosm, the individual the microcosm. We would be bolder still and declare that the individual is the universe writ small. This is surely true so far as the control of things being given up to the creative power of the subjective mind is concerned; for our individual subjective mind should be conceived of as our personal share in the universal mind.

The likeness of God in which man was created implies all this. What different interpretations have been given to that declaration! We hardly know what it means. But we are sure it implies a gracious divine equipment that differentiates us from the lower animal creation. Speaking religiously, it means a soul was imparted, divine character-istics inbreathed, a receptivity to the incoming of the Creator's life produced, that we reflect His truth, that in all the future of existence spirit with spirit might meet and commune, that man might be God's child.

But all through the ages God has been created in man's likeness, and always in keeping with the ignorance or intelligence of the human creating mind. We moderns, with all our enlightenment, find it difficult to conceive of Him as other than a large man upon a throne, and far away, because our mean idea of ourselves will not permit the conception of unity and friendliness God desires us to hold.

The Bible encourages this anthropomorphic idea. It refers to Him as guiding us with His hand, protecting with His arm, hearing with His ear, seeing with His eye, inclining toward us with His heart or body. When the mind seeks to give up this finite idea, it often takes refuge in pantheism, and renounces His personality.

Then think of the creedal conceptions of deity, the passions, for instance, that Calvanism has endowed Him with, relentless, revenging, eternally punishing the unfortunate, unrepenting soul.

Now, in the last analysis, whether we create God in our likeness, or think of ourselves as created in His, this new psychologic revelation of the power of the subjective mind helps out. There can not be anything creative and remedial in the finite that is not conceived of as resident also in the infinite. And the creative power of the universal mind, since science has discovered similar power in the individual mind, must be the fulness of that lesser manifestation which results from the individual's creation in God's likeness.

What consciousness of power does such conviction give. The marvelous intelligence underlying the whole creation is inherent in every one of nature's manifestations, and preeminently inherent in ourselves. Every advance in science consists in discovering new intricacies in and between the atoms that make up this magnificent universal order, which need only to be recognized to be brought into practical use. Divine intelligence crops out everywhere. The entire life principle is charged with it.

How came our earth, with all its teeming life, into existence? Our planet's history stands first an incandescent nebula spread over vast infinitudes of space. Then it condenses into a central sun surrounded with glowing planets in all stages of development, each evolved from that plastic primordial matter. Then follow untold millennia of slow geological formation, and the upspringing of all forms of vegetable and animal life, until through a never-ceasing, never-hurrying, majestic forward movement creation is fitted for man's residence. Then he appears, a spark of intelligence out of the infinite light, born with equipment that enables him to cooperate with God in carrying out the divine designs into all truthful and beautiful realizations.

Jesus postulated it all when He said, "God is Spirit." The writer of Genesis said the same when he exclaimed, "In the beginning God." That wonderful description of creation which follows the sublime declaration may not be scientific, but it is true nevertheless, simply, strongly, beautifully true, because it ascribes it all to God. It shows concisely that all visible things must have their origin in God, who is spirit, with intelligence, its supreme characteristic—an intelligence filled with thought-images. Every one is an ideal pattern to be worked out in some created thing. No other occupation for spirit can be conceived than the production of thought-images, prior to its manifestation in matter. These thought-images or ideas are what Plato of old referred to in his theory of ideas when he mentions them as infinite models which God contemplates and actively directs unto the creation of all finite order and beauty.

All nature, then, is pervaded with ideas of the good, the beautiful, the true. And for animate nature it is an ideal of health, harmony, wholeness. The animal existence realizes this much more universally than the human. They enjoy as man does not. They are at one with inward and outward conditions. The universal life is admirably tho not fully embodied there. Why should man, the highest expression of this life, be so out of sorts in every department of his nature? Well, because of both actual and ideal considerations. He is made in God's image. God's very being, an infinite actuality is the idea that is to be worked out in him. Hear the sublime command, "Be ye perfect as your Father in heaven is perfect." What a contract has God upon His hands! What an infinite undertaking has man!

Then when you realize the odds against which the struggle must be waged! What separates humanity from the life universal, with all its rich wholeness, is volition. Because in God's image, he is endowed with power of choice. That is the great divisional force which makes for realization of selfhood, but alas! also for independence. All the universe of God is his to share, all the resourcefulness of nature his to claim. He draws upon it all, each moment of his living, appropriates all natural blessings, and when he can, he puts a wall around it and calls it his. His selfishness, his incessant striving, make everything wrong. Bound to bend everything to himself, he encounters obstacles, blunders into difficulties, endures friction, experiences manifold ills—all this in the vain attempt to be independent, foolishly thinking that independence is strength. But he can't embody all the centrifugal forces. He must be played upon by the centripetal forces too. He must, like the star, be held in his orbit. He must respect the all-comprehensive law of compensation.

Let us hope that he, after seeing the fruitlessness and emptiness of such low striving, learns his lesson and fits into the plan of God. Now, the very equipment, that superb volitional power which served him ill in separating him from the all-power of God, shall serve him well in enabling him to make the necessary connections with the infinite supply. He fits himself into the divine plan, he chooses life. God's creative power is a recreative power too, ready and glad to enter into every little human receptive doorway. Man's whole being may be made whole and harmonious and at ease. The very will power that seemed to be his curse will prove his blessing now. It puts him in touch with that boundless storehouse of life and good we call nature. He has within his grasp the key to all its treasures. His mental ability is that key. Whatsoever he asks for, in faith believing, he shall receive. For nature is not dead uniformity of law, but all alive with creative and curative life-power, the life-power of the infinite God.

To do this we must picture the universal mind as the ideal of all we could wish it to be, both to ourselves and all the great world of mortals. Accompanying this must be the strong desire to reproduce this ideal, however imperfectly, in our life. Then can we cheerfully contemplate this divine remedial life-force as our ever-present friend, furnishing us with all good, guarding us from all selfish excesses, guiding us unto all beneficence and enrichment of experience.

How splendidly the life of Christ looms up out of the distance of the years amidst such contemplation! Well may He be called the ideal man! You keep within rational bounds when you also call Him the perfect man. Just as it is impossible for the artist to conceive of Him as other than of beautiful countenance, Jewish rather than Grecian tho He was, so of His life—strong of body and never ill; pure of soul and never for an instant of impure thought; powerful in his convictions, thinking and speaking accurately, truthfully;

[158]

always at one with the divine life principle, and in harmony with God. Thus He was neither thinker nor student. He never sat at the feet of the learned Gamaliel—nor did He need to do so. On the other hand, He confounded the rabbis, and at the inconspicuous age of twelve seems to have been able to hold His own with priests in the temple. A precocious child, exclaims the world! Yes, assuredly that, and along all lines. Nature flashes some genius into the youth both through the creative universal and the creative individual intelligence, and a Shakespeare becomes eminent in dramatic art, a Mozart in music, a Raffael in painting and a Michelangelo in sculpture, but Christ's genius was preeminently spiritual, and was the great constitutional center of his life. Mentally, it was intuition, the very comprehending vision of truth. Morally, it was perfect divine rectitude in thought and act. Spiritually His life was completely *en rapport* with God. And so intimately familiar was He with the infinite mind that he was conscious of no incongruity of thought in ascribing to God all love and calling Him Father. No wonder He called Himself the way, the truth, the life. Man needs no more perfect guide into the best living here or to the eternal life that is supposed to lie beyond the stars.

I spoke recently of the perfect atonement between the conscious and subconscious minds of Jesus, claiming it was back of any subsequent atonement He achieved. A ministerial friend, noticing the statement, stated that he preferred to think of Christ's power having its source in God rather than in His own subconscious life. It was my friend's kindly criticism that gave rise to this sermon, to show that even in us the subjective mind is a part of the universal subjective mind in which all creative and remedial power dwells. If true of us imperfect men, it is preeminently true of Jesus. Consciously and unconsciously He was full of spirit, full of the divine creative and curative power that could manifest itself even in the calling of the dead to life.

I think there will have to be some new theology written of a Christological nature—a theology that grounds itself in less mechanical views of incarnation than that of the virgin birth, and in truer more comprehensive theory of atonement than any yet formulated. Isn't it in our zeal for formulation that all our trouble lies? Is there not always danger in striving to put any eternal truth into a finite concept, danger of missing the point you seek to express? Truth is too subtle and elusive to be caged in human speech. Better see it in the large, tho vaguely. Better follow humbly in its shining trail. Better just show the student who desires to know, how he can let it into his life than strive after satisfactory explanation or to express it cut and dried in formula.

Be content, then, to let Jesus remain largely inexplicable, unless you catch His self-revealing simplicity. See Him as the ideal man, because all necessary example of what we unideal men should pattern after. Be sure He was no less practical for being ideal. How He lived our life! How He was identified with our experiences! How He carried health, forgiveness, redemption and God's good cheer into homes and lives! You notice I put health first, because He put it first. It looks as tho He intended it should always be kept first. He seems to have been so anxious to banish human abnormal restrictions and free the life of all unnecessary entanglements that He was friendly to all human ills in whatever department of the individual nature they might be.

The truth underlying it all is that the individual is intended to be a cosmos as truly as is the universe. And tho it seems a misinterpretation of God's thought to say so, yet I believe it true that He is more anxious that the individual universe be complete and healthy and harmonious through and through than the external universe. Is it not true that the life of man can reflect His glory as the universe can not? It is an intelligent, affectionate, volitional homage the individual life can give. The universe is only man's home. The limitless soul of man is God's home. His inconspicuous body is designated His temple beautiful. Why not, then, a healthful, cheerful, pure, and righteous man as God's chief concern? Thus the latent health-producing possibilities of power within His life. Thus also the God-created, health-producing universe without.

But alas, how alarming a chaos is man, spirit, mind, heart, and body sick, ill with error, superstition, selfishness, and what we mortals call disease, restricted, crowded, supprest with a polluting, narrowing environment that never wearies of sending worry into the mind and sickness into the body, and keeps the renovating light of God's countenance crowded out!

That is why Christianity is here, a living, reconstructive reality, to show us the way of God. And, remember, it is unto the Church's keeping that Christianity is given. We of the Church are appointed to propel it into all the abodes of men as a curative saving force. But if the light within thee be darkness; if the salt hath lost its savor, this is why the hope of the Church is not in conserving its ecclesiastical order, its creedal tenets, the sanctity of its sacred rites, but in missionary endeavor, first, midst, and last. When the Church loses this evangelizing zeal, it loses its vitality, ceases to be fruit-bearing, and like the barren fig-tree, becomes a cumberer of the ground.

A strange phenomenon has arisen lately.

It is that Christianity has sprung up, and is flourishing outside the Church. Not creedal, not doctrinal, not fully Biblical, but practical, helpful, remedial, nevertheless. I refer to multitudinous, so-called, New Thought classes that are claiming attention. A weak name for a strong reality! They at least endeavor to put man in possession of himself bodily, mentally, and succeed. They even make him acquainted with the remedial power of God for heart and spirit, too; quite unscientific, as is Christian Science, also; quite partially Scriptural.

But they win the troubled diseased masses whom the Church has failed to hold because it was more intent upon bolstering up an ecclesiastical institution than in redeeming men, redeeming them with a full, rich, present redemption for every department of their natures.

So eminent an observer as Dr. Newman Smyth notes this condition and deplores it in his recent book "The Passing Protestantism." "The Protestant churches," he exclaims, "are not maintaining their influence over considerable areas of thought. It is not simply that worldliness and unbelief are coming in; but much religion is withdrawing from the churches. In almost any community there may be found considerable numbers of people who are not in their habits of mind irreligious nor without faith in their hearts, but they belong to no church, confess no creed, and rarely attend public worship. They may seek after new cults, or remain content with feeling themselves to be religious in general, with no beliefs in particular. There is a kind of religious literature not generally known among our church-membership, seldom recognized by theologians, but to be found in the book-stores and having large sales, a literature somewhat mystical, quietistic and spiritual, but neither churchly nor very distinctively Christian.

"The growth and spread of this kind of literature outside the domain of the Church is a noteworthy phenomenon of the times in which we live. The older mysticism, the former quietism, flourished within the Church. Now it springs up largely outside the churches and beyond their creeds."

And even the stage is vying with the

Church along this line. Within a few years many plays have been staged taking advantage of this new psychologic revelation of the curative power in the subjective self. It seems to have found attractive embodiment, indeed, in that play, ''The Servant in the House,'' which is, perhaps the most astounding conception ever staged, for we are at first shocked to find that servant in the house pictured in quite unmistakable terms as Jesus Christ. But how He cleanses the house wherein He is a servant! How His silent influence is made to radiate, transforming truth-convictions into a bishop's life on the one side and into a tramp's life on the other, until their lives are devoted through that Christ presence in the house to the true redemption of humanity!

I have found one of the most startling revelations of my ministerial life in the transformed personalities of two social friends, a husband and wife, both brought up in the Church, but both not consciously helped thereby. Nevertheless, to-day they stand with truth-filled hearts, God-illumined minds, and joyous faces, and with a deep affection for

Jesus Christ. But it all came from sources outside the Church. Not through the theater; do not mistake the source. The theater is nine-tenths demoralizing, and the whole ten worldly and mercenary. It teaches sometimes a moral lesson, but it never recreates a life, nor imparts truth, unto the reconstruction of character, nor leads a soul to God. But the pity of it that men and women find not in the Church the power they crave for living, but feel constrained to seek it through outside means. The Church is the God-appointed way of worship, tho we should not be so prejudiced as to say that man can not worship God save in the Church.

Jesus taught us differently centuries ago. Neither on this mountain nor at Jerusalem—where the temple stood—is His word to the Samaritan woman, but they that worship God must worship Him in spirit and in truth. There was that outcast soul journeying day after day to Jacob's well for the water to quench her thirst. And there sat the stranger on the well-curb who offered her the water of life that would spring up within her unto life eternal. That and the accompanying word upon what constituted worship are the revelations the Church must introduce to all the world. Such worship wherever engaged in, tho the Christian Church is naturally the soul's trysting-place, opens all the avenues of the life to the incoming tides of the spirit that cleanse, pardon, illumine, and revitalize the life.

VI

DEMANDING HEALTH

All things whatsoever ye pray and ask for, believe that ye hath received them, and ye shall receive them.—New Testament Scriptures.

Yea manhood hath a wider span and larger principle of life than man.
For soul inherits all that soul would dare;
>   —James Russell Lowell.

Self-reverence, self-knowledge, self-control—these three alone lead life to sovereign power.
>   —Tennyson.

Who is the true man? He who does the truth and never holds a principle on which he is not prepared in any hour to act and in any hour risk the consequences of holding it.
>   —Carlyle.

Man needs the ideal even more than he needs bread. The ideal is the bread of the soul.
>   —Edwin Markham.

VI

DEMANDING HEALTH

Scholarship and faith—Scriptural encouragement in demanding health—The marvels of faith—Our right as God's children to enjoy God's health-giving spirit as much as all other forms of nature—Afraid to demand—Everything making incessant demands on us—Suggestion's power over the universal mind—Getting what you want—Every thought-ideal a magnet that draws intelligence, moral life, and physical health.

A REMARKABLE statement is that word of Jesus, "All things whatsoever ye pray and ask for believe that ye hath received them and ye shall receive them." But we are indebted for it to the Christian scholars who in revising the New Testament tucked the assuring word into the margin of their manuscript. Verily, scholarship reveals more than it conceals. How alarmed we were a few years ago that revising the Scriptures meant explaining them away; exploding their mysteries, impairing their genius, invalidating their force. To the unenlightened mind form and force are closely allied, as also is mystery and ignorance. Only intelligence sees form to restrict force, enlightenment to conserve mystery. Sharpened faculty and education achieve that, and discover much more mysterious and latent energy in living truth than ignorant minds steeped in formal and mechanical conclusions dream exist. The Scriptures are living truth, in which resides a quickening spirit. Blest scholarship, that uncovers both the truth that lives and the spirit that quickens to the realization of men. Investigation never explains anything away worth retaining. Science is never the enemy of truth. If it breaks up the formal and tears down the superstitious, it is only that it may reveal facts that were before concealed.

That is why scholarship and science are friendly to faith. Discovering its vitality, they herald it to the world. As the substance of the thing hoped for, the evidence of the thing not seen, faith was well worth possessing. But when the scholars flash their scrutiny upon it nothing short of personal assurance and spiritual conviction can express its realistic traits. Thus the revisers translate that ancient passage in the most vital terms conceivable when they affirm that faith is the assurance of the thing hoped for, the conviction of the thing not seen. There also, in the passage before us, they enhance the vitality and realism of faith in making the reality asked for identical with its possession. Faith is not only asking but believing that you have received. Only such assured, convinced souls can expect to receive. Do you not see why the conviction of having already received is represented as implied in the asking, rather than with the realization of the receiving which is to be ours in the future? There's the secret of the entire problem.

Yet how simple to the trusting soul. You are asking God. That explains it all. You have complied with the conditions that put His infinite power at your disposal. Every faculty of that divine creating and recreating personality, mind, will and heart, are in perfect accord and yours to command. Only be reverent and as simple as a little child and all things are yours, so Jesus said.

Yes, I know, it is too good to be true. Too easy to be appreciated. Thus the same finite

thought that conceives of God as far away
and inaccessible seems to delight to think of
Him as demanding constant sacrifice and un-
ceasing supplication; and even then bestow-
ing His blessings grudgingly, and calmly and
coldly waiting for some better day than now.
Such description comes dangerously near describing our faith. No wonder mountains
are never moved into the midst of the sea.
No wonder we get no comfort out of our
religion. No wonder our sorrows are never
eradicated, our sicknesses never healed. We
not only have no faith, but, sadder still, we
have not yet found out what faith is. We
ask. How zealously we ask. But the noise
we are all the while making by the asking
prevents us from being still long enough to
know that He is God. We believe He is able
to bless. But no thanks to us for even that
poor compliment to the all-loving, all-powerful God. It can hardly be counted virtue on
our part, for it was not deliberately acquired.
We were brought up that way. We may go
so far as to believe He will bless us in His
own good time and if our request be in keeping with His will.

But believe me Lord Tennyson would never have given us that immortal outburst concerning prayer had he been so feebly inspired:

More things are wrought by prayer than this world dreams of,
Therefore let thy prayers rise like a fountain for me night
    and day,
For what are men better than sheep or goats
That nourish a blind life within the brain,
If, knowing God they lift not hands of prayer
Both for themselves and those who call them friend.
For so the whole round earth is every way
Bound by gold chains about the feet of God.

Nor would Sir Thomas Moore have exclaimed,

As down in the sunless retreats of the ocean,
Sweet flowers are springing no mortal can see,
So deep in my soul the still prayer of devotion,
Unheard by the world, rises silent to Thee.

Nor would our Lord have said:

.   Ask and ye shall receive.

Nor would the Apostle Paul have written:

Pray without ceasing.

All these spell intimacy, assurance, and spiritual daring that are sublime.

So timorous are we lest we claim too much. And all the while our false sense of propriety, and our timorous attitude, erroneously named reverence, are nothing more positive than lack of assurance in the thing we ask and hope for, nothing better than lack of confidence in both the God prayed to and the reality unseen. Our many peradventures hedge us in and fence God out. Ask till doomsday, but you ask amiss. Believe till doomsday that God will bless, and you believe amiss. Not until you ask, believing you have received, shall you receive. Otherwise you have no faith.

You must see why this is. Faith is walking in the dark, trusting where you can not see, taking the leap into the distance. God forgive me. Faith is none of these adventures. It only appears to savor of the darkness, the unseeing, the launching forth upon the vague and distant path. Rather is it divinest light and truest vision, and setting our feet firmly upon a safe and near-by way. All this because it is blest, positive God-given assurance and conviction. It is just taking hold of God. It is just appropriating His remedial power for your crying need. It is just applying His infinite resources, which are also your infinite resources, to your spiritual and physical ills.

The trouble is we are too timorous and faint-hearted to make demands upon God in line with our crying needs. This trouble is based on a deeper trouble still. It is that we have no realistic conviction that He is our Father and that we are His children. If we had, there would be more intimacy and confidence between us.

If children stood aloof from their human fathers as do we from God, the household would be a cold, lonely, unfilial, unfatherly abode in very truth. When a child holds such distant relationship, it breaks the parents' hearts. And when the father or mother fails in the affection and care they should bestow the child's face becomes hard and sorrowful.

No wonder that, as children of God, we have no cheer in our faces and joy in our hearts. The divine fatherhood has no positive and helpful meaning for us at all. We repeat it in the creeds. We read it in the Bible. We, parrot-like, let it glide off the tongue. But, alas! we have neither intelligent conception of the glad relationship nor emotional appreciation of the help and uplift of His fatherly presence.

But see how the Bible is all the while calmly, persistently assuring us of His eagerness to give us all good gifts. In Christ's official utterance, the Sermon on the Mount, He exclaims: "Ask, and it shall be given you; seek ye and ye shall find; knock and it shall be opened unto you. For every one that asketh receiveth, and he that seeketh findeth, and to him that knocketh the door shall be opened. What man is there of you whom if his son ask bread will he give him a stone, or if he ask a fish will he give him a serpent? If ye then being evil know how to give good gifts unto your children, how much more will your father which is in heaven give good gifts to them that ask him."

In Luke's portrayal of this same incident there is something of importance added; namely, encouragement to demand of God so persistently refusal on God's part is absolutely out of the question. "Which of you shall have a friend and shall go to him at midnight and say unto him, 'Friend, lend me three loaves, for a friend of mine in his jour-

ney has come to me and I have nothing to set
before him,' and he from within shall answer
and say, 'Trouble me not; the door is now
shut and my children are with me in bed. I
can not rise and give thee.' I say unto thee
he will not rise and give him because he is
his friend, yet because of his importunity he
will rise and give him as many as he
needeth.'' Notice the Master is talking about
physical necessities, loaves of bread. And in
the first quotation it is not stated what we
are to ask and seek for. But it is intimated
through the use of the natural terms, egg and
fish, that it is natural necessities that the
Heavenly Father will give. And even tho,
as in Luke, it be the giving of His Spirit that
is designated, who shall say it is not the spirit
of health and good cheer that the Spirit of
God imparts?

Let nature teach thee how and what God
gives. How confidently the trees are making
demands on God these beautiful sunny days.
As also the grass and flowers and the ivy
climbing up the side of the church where we
are worshiping. Then, too, the animal creation, that it live and enjoy His health-giving

spirit. And how satisfactory is God's response.

Am I trivial, mentioning these commonplace growths? Well, then, hear Jesus say, "Behold the fowls of the air: they sow not, neither do they reap; yet their heavenly Father feedeth them. Are ye not better than they? Consider the lilies of the field, how they grow; yet not even Solomon in all his glory was arrayed like one of these. Wherefore, if God so clothe the grass of the field which to-day is and to-morrow is cast into the oven, shall He not much more clothe you, O ye of little faith?" Ah, beloved! we have not begun to put God to the test to which He is, both in the Bible and in nature, inviting us. We are so humble, you know, and sinful withal. Yes, that is it. And our theology has near driven us to distraction through the emphasis placed on the negative side of things. It is so ponderous and pompous and opinionated.

Our churches have followed theology to the forgetfulness of Scripture, and proclaimed conviction of sin instead of the converting, revitalizing power of the Gospel, so that it is

no wonder the churches are empty and losing
their hold on the masses. But the time will
come when it will be counted a sin to think
of God as a hard taskmaster instead of the
loving Father that He is. The day is not far
off when the greatest sin will be to think of
yourself as a sinner. Once let the God Jesus
has revealed come in, He will drive out every
vestige of the sin that is lurking in your
consciousness and impart the consciousness
of His presence, in which is nothing but
blessing for thy life. Cease thinking of
yourself. Think of God. He is the Father
that thinks nothing but good of thee, and
places at thy disposal the most complete life
equipment conceivable to take the place of
thy ills. Demand health of God for whatever
department of thy nature thou seest to be
sick. Health will come running in to crowd
out sickness and make thy life its dwelling-
place.

We refuse to demand. Our modesty prevents, we say. But our external affairs are
not so modest by half. Everything that exists
makes constant demand on us. And our inherent politeness prevents resentment. Bet-

ter to speak the truth and say that it is our mean opinion of ourselves that bids us yield. We dare neither resist powerful intrusions, nor make worthy demands of the universe to give upbuilding substitutes. No mistake about it, we are a sorry lot.

Everything, I say, makes demand on us. There is heredity. Never a week but what some sick soul offers it as an excuse for its ills. But, sir, you know, I inherited this weakness. Well, then, I answer, in the name of God, overcome it and be strong. Every one of us has the power. The weakest soul in existence can be stronger than heredity, so far as inherited moral and physical weakness goes.

Then there is environment, a poor, dead condition, until we vitalize it by identifying our sympathetic personality therewith. Yet what a successful demand it makes.

Then there is disease, demanding entertainment of us, and the moment its bleared face looks in at the window we are more prone to fall under its discouraging influence than to stand up defiantly, and in the name of the living God command it to be gone.

And there are the ravages of time, seeking opportunity to age us before our work is done. We oftener yield than resist, because too actually lazy often to put up a good square fight. The earth is full of men and women that age, as well as become sick, before they should. Yet how assiduously these indolent souls rush, as did Ponce de Leon to the everglades of Florida, or some other supposed health resort, to find the fountain of youth. They forget that it is within, but quite sealed up there, full of stagnant water, because they are too negligent to draw on it for refreshment and health.

All this is what we mean by saying that everything makes demands on us; good things, as opportunity, duty, external suffering and poverty. And how faithfully we respond in sympathy and charity, responsibility and ceaseless endeavor.

But, alas! bad things knock at the door, too—bad if allowed to become a dominating power—heredity, circumstances, business, society, domesticity, time's ravages, age, sickness, death. And we let them in, and tho offering faint protest, vacate the throne for them to usurp it, forgetting all the while that we have a duty to ourselves, a duty to rise up and claim our sovereignty as a child of God.

Let us assert ourselves, our plain, every-day, commonplace selves. There is royal blood in us, commonplace tho we be. We are every one of us children of the King. You wouldn't think so to see us scouting around in the back alleys, subsisting upon the garbage, like so many self-confest prodigals, filling our lives with the husks that the swine eat.

The sad thing about it all is that "the Father," whose loving eye follows us, is ever urging us to assert ourselves against these demoralizing influences. His power is within us, latent there. His encouragements about us pressing on all sides. Through the within power and the without we can, if we will, be strong enough to separate ourselves from the fears, worries, sorrows and sicknesses of the friction-filled earth plain. Easier, however, instead of living on the level and fighting to win, to live upon the plain just above that of the old earth ills, where in the place of the world's friction and grief and that consciousness of weakness that sooner or later leads to discouragement and despair we possess the consciousness of God's presence, which empowers for the enjoyment of all ease and rest and peace.

We have been speaking religiously in all that has been said. Let us express the same in psychologic terms. So much we have made of the power of suggestion, the ability to put cheer ideals and health thoughts into the subconscious depths where remedial powers are waiting to lend their aid to these strong suggestions unto all blest realizations. Remember this individual power is only the manifestation of that universal power that creates and recreates all natural forms which are crowded to the brim with the divine life vigor, else it could not create health in us.

Now for the culminating thought; namely, that we can suggest to the universal creative mind without, as to the creative universal mind within, our need, and the thought ideal that will satisfy that need. Then God will do the rest. The creative mind will furnish all the remedial power needed and desired to make that thought ideal real to the conscious life.

The Scriptures bid us reach this conclusion in simpler speech, asserting that whatsoever we ask, believing we have received, we shall receive. Because God is constantly striving to make all things new. The moment we cooperate with God in such splendid achievement that moment we receive. Why? you ask. Because we have, through our God consciousness, risen to a higher plane than that of nature, even to the absolute, which is not conditioned by time and space, or any adverse contingencies whatsoever. That is why asking is receiving. We have become laborers together with God. We have climbed up into the realm of God's good will.

You know what the nature of the magnet is. How it draws the steel filings to itself until they cling there as if claiming affinity with that attracting magnetized steel. Thought is the most magnetic power in all existence. God's sympathetic atmosphere carries it over the continents and across the seas. It leaps across all distances. It penetrates all fast-nesses. It claims its own midst all restricted circumstances. It is an all-powerful thought propulsion, hence travels faster than lightning's speed.

That thought ideal of your need intensified by your desire is a spiritual magnet that attracts the realities you crave. Is it intelligence you demand? Is your mind sluggish? Is it difficult to concentrate your attention on the work you do, the book you read, the problem you solve? Make your demand. Concentrate it in the intense ideal you send out into the universal reality. It is the strong, sharpened, comprehensive intelligence you would possess. The universe, which is full of intelligence, will serve you. That sent-out thought becomes a very center of attraction that draws to itself the intelligence you demand. Believe that the asking is the receiving, and you shall receive, because you have asked of God.

Is it moral strength you want? Are the temptations upon the plane of your daily living stronger than are you? Reverse the conditions. Become more assertive than the evil pulling you down. Launch your moral thought ideal out into the silence where God is. Believe you have received because you have asked, and you shall receive, because you ask of God, who, Jesus tells us, is more willing to give good gifts to His children than is earthly parent, who never gives a serpent for a fish, or a scorpion for an egg, or a stone for bread. Will not He who furnishes the lilies of the field, and the fowls of the air with all needed food, much more furnish you with the spirit needed to make you morally whole? O ye of little faith.

So of health. The universe is full of it because charged with the life of God. Demand it, and you will receive it, for that is faith. It is your due as God's best creation, as your Father's trusting, needy child. The trouble with us is we do not feel at home in our Father's presence. We do not realize that we are spirits in potentiality as Infinite as is God. Our consciousness needs to be enlarged and heightened sufficiently to claim our privilege to live in an infinite thought world of cheer, purity and confidence in the All Father that all is well. How beautifully has Browning, theologian, religionist and poet all in one, exprest this idea:

> For what is Infinite must be a home,
>   A shelter for the meanest life,
> Where it is free to reach its greatest growth,
>   Far from the reach of strife.
> We share in what is Infinite, 'tis ours;
>   For we and it alike are Thine.
> What I enjoy, great God, by right of Thee
>   Is more than doubly mine.

Strange, isn't it, that the Church has through all the centuries put the far-away interests first, and made the hardest easiest to attain? It has even taught that eternal life may be had for the asking, becoming a present consciousness to the individual. It has done well. The Master said, "Seek first the kingdom of God and all these things shall be added unto you." The Church has put the emphasis in the right place, I say, but it has left the other things that should be added to take care of themselves. It has not claimed its own for its redeemed constituency. It has not made the easier, nearer demand, so contented has it been in realizing the harder and more remote. Christ never neglected man's most immediate interests, but made the whole man well, distributing physical as well as spiritual ease whenever the opportunity occurred.

Catch the hint. Follow where He leads and dispense physical, moral and spiritual good cheer everywhere.

VII

REALIZING HEALTH

In Him we live and move and have our being.—NEW TES-
TAMENT SCRIPTURES.

*The Eternal God is thy refuge and underneath are the
everlasting arms.*—OLD TESTAMENT SCRIPTURES.

*Of all the teachings that which presents a far-distant God
is nearest to absurdity. Either there is none or He is nearer
to every one than our nearest consciousness of self.*
—GEORGE MACDONALD.

*Oh, the little birds sang east, and the little birds sang west,
And I smiled to think God's greatness flowed around our
    incompleteness,
Round our restlessness, His rest.*
—MRS. BROWNING.

VII

REALIZING HEALTH

The new outlook upon life—Living daily in the presence of God—The new optimism and what it accomplishes in terms of health—Living in everything else except God—The self-assertion that dare demand for itself all good, and command the departure of all evil and disease—A present *versus* an unknown and absentee God—Does commanding good to come, and evil to go, really work? —Some instances of such working in alcoholism, immorality, obsession, dread of disease, hysteria.

WE are standing on advanced ground these days. But only because we have entered into that consciousness where we dare claim our rights as children of God. We no longer hedge ourselves about with the self-imposed conditions of peradventures and ifs, even the if of His will. Knowing that will, and desirous that it should be done on earth as in heaven, we bend every faculty of the soul to its realization. We used to bear our ills patiently enough, believing "that tribulation worketh patience and patience experience and experience hope, and that hope maketh not ashamed." We believe it no less in asserting ourselves against tribulation's control. But we demand grace enough to bear our ills patiently, and have an experience in which His presence is reflected, and a hope that so savors at times of blest realization that it is kept healthy and strong.

So of sympathy. If deliverance from our ills makes us so self-contained that we sympathize no longer with another's misfortune, better no deliverance at all. True, sympathy could not be but for the immense dark background of personal suffering that evolves it into existence. But that the life picture be worth the artist's skill the individual soul must stand out from that background in clear, strong lines. Otherwise, it is foreground. The divine power is needed that the man emerge therefrom and stand forth strong enough both to sympathize with those whose individualities are lost in the dense darkness of the background, and to help forward those who are struggling to the front.

Fear not that you will lose an iota of the sanctifying benefit of patience, or the exhilaration of hope, or the softening influence of sympathy, or the richness of experience through deliverance from tribulation and the sweet consciousness of resting in the invigorating health-realized life of God. At the top of the mountain you have all you possest on the plains, or at any stage of the upward climb, and an unsurpassed view besides. Spiritual life never minimizes manhood. Every incoming tide of the Spirit increases quantitatively and qualitatively manhood's worth.

You see, we are simply emphasizing a new approach to life. We have caught a nearer vision of God. We have felt the thrill of a more present relationship with the All Father than we ever dreamed we could have this side of the stars. All that we are now realizing we were content to hold in abeyance until as disembodied spirits we reached that far-off realm where the wicked cease from troubling and the weary are at rest. But precious revelation that we are to-day as much the children of God as we ever will be; that He loves us as fondly as He ever can; that time and space are not hampering conditions to the incoming of His eternal life vigor, and that altho it does not yet appear what we shall be, nevertheless that He is as interested in filling this flesh-and-blood body of ours with health as He will be in any spirit body we may inhabit in the far-away eternities.

Having such conviction, how can we think of Him longer as an unknown God? We used to be as ignorant of His nearness and helpfulness as were those Athenians to whom Paul spoke. Yes, we were religious. So were they. We erected our altars, formulated our beliefs, offered our sacrifices, prayed our prayers. But how far away He was! A majestic being upon a throne, as cold as majestic; having mercy where He would have mercy, condemning where He chose. We tried to please Him, sought out His laws, attempted compliance with His commandments, and hoped, often against hope, that somehow, through the merits of Jesus, we would be saved. But it was mechanical, the spirit in us was heavy, the face expressionless, and with an awful sense of loneliness in the heart.

We never said with Professor Clifford that the Great Companion was dead. We didn't dare to. Better reason still. He never really seemed alive, and only live things die. We conceded all we had been taught about His existence. But He was as dead as an Egyptian mummy, so far as receiving any conscious, positive spiritual energy from Him went. And all the while it was written on the sacred page that in Him we lived and moved and had our being. Even the Old Testament was declaring that the eternal God was our refuge and underneath were the everlasting arms.

Inspirations flash at times from unexpected places. No jewel ever scintillated light more radiantly than do these passages of Holy Writ. The writer of Deuteronomy is describing Moses' farewell address to the tribes of Israel, when this comforting word flashes forth. Paul intends nothing more than an argument in behalf of repentance when this truth escapes him. But the inspirations of God become crystallized in some clear word or other, and become imprinted upon a parchment, else enter a human heart and get remembered long after the historical situation that called them forth is forgotten, and the entire life experience is richer in consequence.

Everything worth possessing follows from this sublime conception. The individual belongs to the universal. All mischief results in separation. Self-consciousness, to the shutting out of God consciousness, is sin. It is also loneliness, sickness, hardness of heart, leanness of soul and depression of spirit. But once see that man's home is in God, once have the consciousness of nestling closely into the everlasting arms, supporting, resting, strengthening, protecting; then all is well. That is what it means. No human frailty that can not be strengthened. No heart-sickening despondency that can not be invaded and overthrown with joy. No feverish restlessness that shall not settle down in the holy calm of quietude and peace.

How easy now to be optimistic. The pessimist is he who credits no worthy foundation to this surging, storm-tossed, perplexed existence. He judges by appearances. Surface impressions are his only data. He has no perception of fundamentals. He has never caught a glimpse of this comforting word underneath. The optimist builds his world construction upon that all-sufficient thought. The apparent, the phenomenal, the superficial, can not beguile him. He reads between the lines. He sees under the form. He relies on God. Underneath! How far? The thought suggested by that word is immeasurable. No human plummet ever sounded its shining depths. It is a conception not to be measured, but to be relied upon.

It is such a term as the opening verse of Genesis, also of the Gospel of St. John, contains: "In the beginning, God." How far back? Back of all our conclusions, our estimates, our conceptions, our thoughts. Back beyond all our hopes and fears, our aspirations and disappointments. Back even of all creation, even of the first faint glimmer suggestive of created things. In the beginning. Underneath. The one is as immeasurable as the other. Down under all our fret and worry, our thought and striving, what we are, or even shall become, is God. In the beginning and underneath are only longer and more definite ways of spelling God. The optimist is he who gets back of and under all the perplexity and contradiction of appearances to God.

Hereafter we have an unfailing encouragement for work. What kind shall we engage in? That which God can bless. That which the everlasting arms can consistently support. How much shall we do? It would seem a great deal. Our enthusiasm based on such assurance would sanction much. But it is quality rather than quantity of work that counts. It is when left to ourselves that the trouble begins. Seeing so much to do, and so little time for achieving, we toil, and strain, and become fretful and nervous, and with little else than failure for our pains. But relying upon the divine embrace restricts our efforts. We become conscious of better things to live for than incessant toil. His will, not ours, becomes the incentive. His strength, not ours, becomes our joy. We become receptive, a free channel for the divine life purpose to flow through. Work indeed to be done, but cooperative energy now, and achieved through the power omnipotent, omniscient, omnipresent, underneath, above, around. His arms are so strong and large, ours so small and weak. We can embrace and comprehend so little. He can embrace and comprehend so much.

Hereafter we have a blest inspiration to faith—faith in the everlasting arms. They are holding us. Could we rely upon and have access to only so much of God as we could lay hold on, we would know Him very imperfectly, for in our poor finiteness we can grasp so little. It is God's hold on us that counts. Then, our hold on God is fickle. In sorrow we cling to Him tenaciously. But when the grief lifts, we relax our hold to grasp earthly realization, so changeable are we in our affections, so uncertain in our allegiance. We take on the complexion of our circumstances. God seems far away because we doubt His near-by care. The trouble is that we are far away, because we have Him no more in our consciousness.

The allurements of life have crept in, that vast catalog of temporal realities that are never content to play a part, but try ever to usurp our whole attention, tempting us to a belief in their sufficiency. There, for instance, is personal accomplishment, that culture that seems indispensable to distinguished social position, literary, musical, artistic; excellent in its place. All young people should be versed in the literature of the day, in the history of the race, in the classics, in the melodies, in the arts. But beware of the soul's absorption in these.

Then there is that masculine allurement, business; industrial efficiency becomes the thing to live for. Financial success early and late drives us from the home to the office, and from the office home again. But not to rest. We have not rested for years. "Do not talk of rest," said a business man recently, "while competition is so strong."

But what is our substitute for rest? Diversion. We can not keep still—not long enough to know that we are men, let alone long enough to know that He is God. But out and away again to the club, the theater, for pleasure, made up often half of dissipation. The typical New Yorker is a martyr to such a life as this. He spends his days in earning the dollar, his nights in spending it. No wonder he can not stand the strain. Only a physical Hercules could. No wonder nerves become shattered and complete nervous exhaustion results. A sanatorium claims him, sometimes the asylum, not infrequently the suicide's grave. The craze for wealth sometimes makes a man positively blasphemous. A Christian business man said to me a few months ago: "I am like all the rest, striving for the almighty dollar." There is no hope for a man who sees a dollar to have the Deity's characteristics. Nor for him who allows pleasure to take him up into its arms and run away with him.

Need of such preaching? I should think so. Never since the world was created more than now, for never before have there been such strong inducements to dissipate ourselves among the trivialities of the senses; and on the other hand to lose our composure, because we have lost the conviction of the Eternal Presence. We live and move and have our being in everything but God. Hence distraction, sickness and a longing for death, because we are driven mad.

Precious Christianity indeed that can impress us with the necessity of calling a halt

before it is too late. This it does by remind-
ing us that we are not living up to our best
capacity. We acted as tho we thought we
were mercantile machines and pleasure-lov-
ing slaves. Christianity assures us that we
are living souls with infinite resources of
power within us, and that we are inhabiting
a universe athrill with vital forces that we
can draw on indefinitely to remedy our ills
and create ourselves anew. No longer the
vision of an unknown God, an absentee Deity
so far away and engaged in such momentous
things that His misguided children are left
to stumble about in the dark, but a God
friendly in the extreme. Even so lovingly
and remedially present that we are living,
moving, having our very existence in His sus-
taining watch care. Such is the fundamental
principle that gives inspiration for every
health claim we choose to make. Best of all,
there is no limit that is needed to be considered, inasmuch as there is no limit to the loving resourcefulness of God. Health is our
heritage as God's children, and we can demand it humbly, trustingly, expectantly, and
our demand shall be met.

While we are urged to make demands upon the universal good, I would also have you do some commanding upon the evil that would threaten and oppress you. Both attitudes are expressions of a necessary self-assertion. I mean thought assertion, that the All Father permits His children to use. The Scriptures are full of this necessity for the soul to affirm itself against the world, and in behalf of righteousness. It warns us constantly against letting the world affirm itself against us. "What shall it profit if he gain the world and lose himself." But Christ within you, the hope of glory; the Spirit guidance into the truth; God's loving restraints, and gracious disciplines are all for the enabling of the soul to affirm itself in all strength unto eternal life.

But you ask how shall we send forth our commands upon the evil that would threaten and oppress. By doing it against each intruding ill, as did our Lord against the spirit of evil in the wilderness. I have known more than one person to have done so recently with remedial effect, especially in the case of headache, as well as in cases of nervousness in different forms and conditions of physical lassitude. It is an emphatic form of auto-suggestion, only so definite and direct and conscious that suggestion, which is a hint to the subjective self for its guidance unto desired ends, hardly explains its nature. It is just a direct, positive, imperative command for the malady that afflicts us to begone. "I am a child of God. I will be normal, healthful, easeful. Begone, disturbing, distracting ill." Or as Jesus said to Peter when tempting our Lord from His duty: "Get thee behind me, Satan, thou savorest not of the things that be of God." It is rather astonishing what power we can assert over annoying disturbances by such a strong, volitional command as that. The will is a potent factor in health realizations.

Then how the wise direction of thought upon our maladies achieves for realization of health. This, too, may be thought of as a kind of command for the driving out of ills. In the conscious quiet of His presence concentrate your thought upon your weak or troubled or nervous self, directing the mind as tho external to the body upon the physical spot to be remedied. You have seen a flash-light penetrate the darkness to disclose the objects lurking there. Thought focused upon the different parts of a weak or sluggish body sends vital energy through those parts, which expresses itself in sensations of warmth, or strength or illumination or exhilaration, ac-cording to the remedy desired. The blood's circulation is quickened, and remedial results are realized. And only a few such mental ap-plications covering a few minutes of time are needed for results.

Remember it is as Dr. Schofield has said, "Mind may have its limits, but those limits have never yet been discovered." And as Hudson has said, "That a mental energy ac-tuates every fiber of the body." Believe me there will be marvelous revelations in the fu-ture concerning the ability of both our con-scious and unconscious thought to keep us well, and cure diseases before they are deep set. Perhaps afterward also. But we must first of all become acquainted with ourselves in the ideal and believe in the self's divine integrity as an individualization of the Eternal One in whom resides all life and wholeness.

Horatio Dresser expresses it well when he exclaims: "Have a soul of your own. Be your true self. Think, reflect, realize, until you have a measure of unborrowed conviction which establishes a center of repose, and is a source of happiness and contentment—a center which yields to no outer tumult, but is ever receptive to the divine self; which never harbors fear nor doubt, no matter what the wavering self may say, which never forgets that the individual belongs to the universal, never relaxes its hold of the deepest, truest, most spiritual in life, come what may, be it sorrow, illness or any calamity which life may bring; a center which you will probably discover at last rests on the love of God for its strength, making it a part of eternity and of all power and substance, tho it be but a point in the infinite whole."

But does all this prescription for the realization of health work? Is it practical? Or is it all an evolution of an over optimistic mind, the unfounded vagaries of an overwrought imagination? Does it produce results that are beneficial and worth while? Yes, and enduring withal, besides putting into our keeping the secret for the remedying of future ills.

Ask those who have profest being benefited if it works. Him, for instance, who professes to having been cured of excessive alcoholism, to the complete taking away of the habit that all previous attempted cures have failed to conquer, and who claims that a year hence he will be stronger still against the vice that for twenty years held his life in awful and constant bondage.

Ask him who came with a seeming uncontrollable desire for suicide, induced by forty years' abuse in immorality—mental and physical wreck, despairing, faithless of any cure, and without either ability or desire to work. Hear his exclamation, after five conferences, that he has been greatly benefited and can not come for further treatment as the time spent in further consultation can be better used in finding occupation.

Ask her possest of strange, strong impulses to do a hundred times a day things her reason rebelled against, yet which through threat of dire calamity she yielded to each time. Now she is able to stand up against both the compelling impulse and the threat, and in the name of God and her imperial womanhood defy these demands, and keep a record of her conquests, and each victory brings joy instead of the awful consequences the fear of which held her life in bondage many long, sad years.

And once again ask her, coming from a Western State for treatment, if these principles work. Her fears of disease for thirty years made life miserable, inducing sleeplessness by night and through the day loss of appetite, incessant dread, and blinding tears. So bad was she that after examination a skilled physician said, ''Tho her case is purely mental, I would not touch it were I you, for she is hopeless and the time expended on her will be lost.'' Now she rests in the consciousness of God's protecting care, believing, as she could not before, that all her fears are groundless. Rejoicing that in Him she lives and moves and has her being, and that underneath are the everlasting arms.

And not a few are the testimonies that through the public enunciation of these principles in writing and in speech different maladies are remedied—hysteria of many years' standing, melancholia, worry, sleeplessness, distrust of God and man.

The most remarkable instance of all is a case that in point of time preceded all these—in fact, my very first case, one that was thrust upon me before I had any facilities for individual work, or for testing these remedial principles.

A young lady, thirty years of age, pulled my bell. She no sooner began to tell me of her ills than she broke down in uncontrollable hysteria. All attempt to console her was in vain. She could not talk. She could only sob. For two long hours this pitiful condition continued. I had another caller, and wondered what I could do with this young lady in such abject distress. To send her into the street was not Christian. Yet might she not be an impostor playing a part? It was evident that such unaccountable anguish could not be assumed for a purpose. Stranger tho she was, I sent her to a room in my home, where she could be alone and rest. She needed, above all else, quiet.

Two hours or more after this I went to her

and with difficulty learned her sad story. She had come from Pennsylvania to New York ten days before to look for stenography. Being an orphan, her uncle, with whom she lived, was unsympathetic, as many strong men are with nervous people. He taunted her with her condition and thought she could work if she would—all this while she was teaching school, and for seven years. At last desperate, she got together enough funds to reach New York and take a room, hoping for a situation, but looking each day in vain. Her funds ran out. She planned suicide. Friendless, moneyless, a nervous wreck, she sought me out. She did not want to be cured. She had tried mental healing and faith cure and medical help years before, but in vain. She wanted me to send her home again. I said, "What for?" Her answer was, "To die, I suppose; but," she continued, "it would be among friends." I refused her request and said, "It would be wiser to make you well." "Ah, sir," she replied, "if you could, but there is no cure for me." I said, "Will you take what I have to offer?" After much urging she yielded herself to my entreaties, but only after the promise that I would place her in a sanatorium where she could rest.

I applied the principles of this method and prayed with her, leaving her quiet and calm. Some hours after I called her down to the evening meal, urged her to spend the night, rather than go back to her unattractive room. This invitation was at the request of a physician who wanted to watch the case and test the cure. She, to my surprize, preferred to go to her own room, promising to return to Brooklyn at 9 the next morning.

Before going to New York I told her the doctor would try to secure a sanatorium for her to rest in. We secured a room in the King's Daughters' Home, and she knew I was to be responsible for a fortnight's board. The next morning my suspicions were aroused as 9, 10, 11, 12 o'clock came around, but no young lady appeared. At 1 o'clock she came, and if ever I looked into a changed face and a calm, strong life it was then. She said, "I slept soundly from 11 until 6, my first night's sleep for weeks, I rested until 9. I then felt so strong I went in search of a situation." Thanking us for our help and hospitality, she returned to New York to bring her trunk to the new rest home. But, picking up a paper, she saw an "ad.," asking for a mother's helper in another city. She sought out the lady in one of the New York hotels, secured the situation and went with her to Massachusetts.

I have received a most appreciative letter, telling me that with the new hope and courage received she could not bear to think of sitting around in a rest home for two weeks. She also said, "I have, when tired and inclined to become nervous, gone into the silence of my room, laid on my bed and applied the principles you gave me and found immediate relief and calm."

Why shouldn't these principles work? Since confidence, composure, good cheer, rationality and health are ours by divine right to enjoy, more strange 'twould be if we do not realize them than if we do. Since in God we live and move and have our being, more strange it is not to share the joy of such divine residence than to possess that joy. Since the Eternal God is our refuge and underneath us are the everlasting arms, the strange experience is to be longer storm-tossed and crowd-prest and filled with anxious care.

As one has said: "A little child is timid and afraid when he loses sight of his father and feels the crowd press upon him; but let him catch a glimpse of his father, let his father lift him in his arms, and the whole attitude of the child is changed. In perfect confidence he resigns himself to his father's care. The crowd may press upon him now, but he has no fear. He no longer feels the weakness of his own little self. He now partakes of his father's strength. He is one with it. He is for the moment a thing of power. So I, buffeted no longer by the crowd of fears and changing opinions of a soul adrift, resign myself in perfect trust to the care of my Father, conscious of being upheld by the everlasting arms. I can not be otherwise than calm and unafraid."

Emerging from a church one winter Sabbath afternoon, with my little boy, the contrast between the sunlight when we entered and the darkness of the street on coming out was so marked that I said to the little fellow,

"My, isn't it dark; aren't you afraid?" His answer was, as he prest my hand, "I would be if you were not here." So also would we older children be if God were not here. As exclaims the psalmist: "What time I am afraid I will trust in thee." Banish from the human consciousness the doctrine of an unknown and absentee God, and you have gone a long way toward banishing multitudinous human worries, sorrows and sicknesses.

VIII

THE LIGHT OF HIS FACE

Who will show us any good? Lord, lift thou up the light of thy countenance upon us.—OLD TESTAMENT SCRIPTURES.

The Lord bless thee and keep thee. The Lord make His face to shine upon thee and be gracious unto thee, the Lord lift up His countenance upon thee and give thee peace.—OLD TESTAMENT SCRIPTURES.

God's face shines ever upon the dwellers in the Temple Beautiful.
—SWEDENBORG.

Let what is natural in you raise itself to the level of the spiritual, and let the spiritual become once more natural. Thus will your development be harmonious and the peace of heaven will shine upon your brow—always on condition that your peace is made, and that you have climbed your calvary.
—AMIEL'S JOURNAL.

*A presence that disturbs me with the joy
Of elevated thoughts; a sense sublime
Of something far more deeply interfused,
Whose dwelling is the light of setting suns,
And the round ocean and the living air,
And the blue sky, and in the mind of man:
A motion and a spirit that impels
All thinking things, all objects of all thought,
And rolls through all things. Therefore I am still
A lover of the meadows and the woods
And mountains, and of all that we behold
From this green earth—well pleased to recognize
In nature and the language of the sense
The anchor of my purest thoughts, the nurse,
The guide, the guardian of my heart, and soul,
Of all my being.*
—WORDSWORTH.

VIII

THE LIGHT OF HIS FACE

Religion that is worth while—Vital Christianity—The lower
and the higher environments—Turning all natural benefits into blessings of physical and spiritual health—
The Pagan and Christian dependence on Nature—Regarding the air we breathe a conductor of health for our
need—Peace in the face of life's manifold ill-adjustments—Mohammedan and Buddhistic prescriptions, also
Communistic and Socialistic, for seeming peace—
Christ's recommendations in behalf of peace, health,
and good cheer—What the light of His face reveals of
the good, the beautiful, the true.

PRECIOUS counterpart this of what we saw
in the last chapter to be true. If to realize
our life in God, in Whom we live and move
and have our being, is to realize health for
all departments of our nature: what realizations of joy and peace are assured in the
conviction that underneath are the everlasting arms; and that lifted upon us is the light
of His face. It is the consciousness of innumerable intermediary realizations interfering with this sublime conviction that

produces the mischief, bidding us ask the sad question, "Who will show us any good?"

Oh, these interfering intermediaries. What consternation they cause! The gratification of the senses, for instance. The ancient pagan found the good through these. He was quite at home in nature. Sense gratifications were neither interferences nor intermediaries, but welcomed finalities. All he desired was to be let alone to contemplate the universe, and thereby become conscious of the good, the beautiful, the true. This unity of nature is seen in their art. There is no line of separation in the Venus and the Marble Faun between the sensuous centering in nose and mouth and the forehead where the spiritual resides. All features blend into one another suggestive of natural goodness and beauty.

So of their lives. There was no consciousness of being a sinner on the one side, nor of sainthood on the other. But their virtue was centered in the consciousness of what Aristotle called a golden mean of conduct, which spelled a contemplative, easygoing way of living, neither too bad nor too good. It was such contemplation that led Protagoras to exclaim that "man is the measure of all things"; and Socrates to fashion the Greek ideal in this simple maxim "know thyself." But how different from the Christian ideal whose demand is to know God. That immediately opens up a sense of duty, and where that presses the natural senses fail to put our life at ease.

So also differs the Christian from the Greek method of attaining happiness. It is no longer know to be happy, but struggle to be happy, seek to find, strive to enter in at the strait gate. An ever-deepening capacity for happiness is better than happiness itself. Your ability for eternal realization by and by is the most important of all. Thus in Christian art you have the line of separation between the brow where dwells spiritual intelligence, and the lower part of the face where the senses sit enthroned. And the greatest of them all, Michelangelo, was the first to draw that line.

What shall we do, then, to reach unity again? We can not go back to the pagan idea of things. We would not if we could. Our acquaintance with and sense of obligation to God prevent. But we can reach unity through the Christian ideal of ourselves as God's sons and daughters, which the remedial forces of nature shall help us realize.

Then there is our environment. How it hinders instead of serves us, interjecting itself between us and the light of His face. It reminds us that we are creatures of the earth. It bids us deny that we are living souls.. And there we go day after day the rounds of the industrial treadmill; put ourselves upon a par with the lowest of money-getting animals; merge our personalities with the social whirl; seek pleasure laboriously, and after all our pains lose sight of the good, and wonder where it is. We ask always in disgust, often in despair, because our surroundings send us nothing but ill and worry, which generates sickness in the brain cells, and nerve centers, and throughout our entire body. Why don't we draw on God's life forces in order to become strong enough to dominate our surroundings? They should not be allowed to be interferences between the children and the Father.

Then how our very thinking serves us ill. So easy to think evil of things and people, and surroundings, and nature, and God. So hard to think well. So easy to think morbidly and allow abnormal fears and worries to come in. So hard to think cheerily, serenely, healthfully.

You would find it difficult to believe how many unfortunate ones beseech me to lift them out of their fears—fears of God, of disease, of something happening to them, of themselves, of everything that is either powerless to inspire fear, else that is willing to be made positively friendly. They remind me of the legend of the dialogue between the pilgrim and the plague. "Where are you going?" asked an Oriental pilgrim of the plague one day. "I am going to Bagdad to kill 5,000 people," was the reply. A few weeks later the pilgrim met the plague returning. "You told me you were going to Bagdad to kill 5,000 people," said he, "but instead you killed 50,000." "No," said the plague, "I killed only 5,000 as I said I would. The others died of fright."

"The fault, dear Brutus," as Shakespeare

said, "is not in our stars, but in ourselves, that we are underlings." Yes, that is the difficulty. Our false idea of facts and conditions and our weak thinking about them endows them with a harmful, fright-inspiring vitality, and we are by that very act become an underling, piteously asking as we squirm under the gloom of it all, "Who will show us any good?"

We can not see any good until we see with the spirit's vision. Then we credit divine purpose and wise provision and loving care. But only because we are what Trine calls in tune with the Infinite, because we have asked God to lift upon us the light of His face.

I go into your home, and upon the centertable is a piece of fancy needlework with its wrong side uppermost. What a wilderness of cross-stitches greets the eye; what a maze of loose, shaggy ends; what a mass of confusion. Did I not believe you were an intelligent, purposeful being, how disappointed with your waste of time I would be. But I know there is beauty of design on the other side and evidences of intelligent care, a well-thought-out and wrought-out realization

of "worth while" which will reward my faith
in you.

So of creation and existence. The light of
God's face shining into human intelligence
always reveals the good. In that shining we
refuse to be beguiled by appearances. They
bewilder and confuse us unless we recognize
in them the wrong side of eternal reality, but
necessary nevertheless. The mischief is in
making it the right side, the only side, and
refusing to believe in the divine design and
the wealth of enriching realization being
worked out through it all. How apparent is
all this when we share the divine intelligence,
when we become sympathetically at one with
the God of things as they are.

Who will show us any good? The light of
His face flashes upon the problems of nature,
the mysteries, perplexities, contradictions of
existence, and reveals the good, as does the
electric flash-light blaze a path through the
midnight darkness for the ship's prow. That
divine illumination shows the good to be
evolved out of our personal obedient relationship with Him. All things work together
for good—not to the careless observer, nor to

the anxious thinker, but to those trusting souls that love God.

The same light needed to reveal the good is essential to the possession of peace. How precious is its promise to the human heart, and if we can carry about with us the assurance that He who promises is able to fulfil, we have a tolerable degree of satisfaction in spite of our ills, and a blessed incentive for all the future work of life. You must have wondered often why there is so much turmoil and strife among mortals, and why a wise and loving God has not so ordered our existence that health, contentment and joy may be more accessible than they are. Mr. Ingersoll used to delight in telling his audiences that if he were God he would make health, laughter and joy catching instead of sickness, sorrow and tears. But he never got beneath the surface of things enough to detect the underlying causes of this adverse side of life, and suggest a wise and sufficient remedy.

Life's turmoil springs out of life's ill-adjustment. Were there harmony between our life and the relations that constitute our world there would be peace. Confliction, ill-adjustment confront us everywhere.

There is that source of ill-adjustment between you and yourself. Stevenson's famous book set the two natures of man forth in glaring colors when he gave us that psychological study of Dr. Jekyll and Mr. Hyde. The one embodiment showed us at our best, the other at our worst. The one an angel of virtue and helpfulness, the other a demon of cupidity and lust. But it is not necessary to picture man at his best and worst that the struggle be appreciated. It is only necessary to see man as he is and as he ought to be. Every life is composed of an actual and an ideal self. The actual may be a good as truly as a bad self. It is nevertheless a commonplace self, but the ideal self lures us on. How difficult to reach your ideals. Were there more harmony between these two selves there would be more peace.

Then what about confliction between you and your environment? The world is not conducive to our ease. Success is difficult of attainment. In all trades, businesses, professions there are more failures than successes.

Then how near impossible to search for and overtake the fleeting goddess happiness, ever leading us a hopeless chase. Only he who beguiles both himself and happiness with the thought that he cares not an iota for its possession succeeds in being happy. Make another happy and happiness will cast its beneficent influence over your path as well. But how hard to make others happy. How difficult to do your duty to God and fellow man. The mortal soul still chases this will-o'-the-wisp and has only that thin poor thing pleasure for his pains, and tho excellent as diversion and relaxation, yet as controlling pursuit it is always enervating and debasing, and the ill-adjustments between us and the world are increased.

Then the ill-adjustment between ourselves and God. His will is seldom pleasing. We are not God-centered. Self-seeking is our inspiration. Whether we yield cheerfully, or by force, we do not understand God. His mysterious providences are poorly explained. It is a great exclamation point we write after His every act. Why this? Why that? Why this affliction to the home? Why this sickness in my life? We do not understand Him. We are not at one with Him. A dark outlook indeed for a life of peace.

Wherein is the remedy? Men's remedial prescriptions are many and inadequate. Let the old religions assist in solving the first problem. How get rid of the ill-adjustment between the actual and the ideal self? Easy enough, exclaims Mohammedanism. Deny your ideal self. Live in the actual. It is the only real. Be courageous. Conquer by the sword for Allah. If you fall, especially realistic rewards are yours yonder. Your actual self will live midst all conceivable delights. The heaven of Mohammedanism is upon the level of the life that now is, and consists in intensity of carnal or actual realization. Until that heavenly consummation dawns, it is a stolid, all-sufficient peace by simply getting rid of the ideal self, thus rid of the confliction arising therefrom.

The Buddhist goes to the other extreme. "Get rid of your actual self, lose yourself in the ideal," is its cry. Life is evil. There is no remedy for its ills except in getting rid of the life that contains them. Therefore

[229]

Nirvana, all souls losing themselves in the all-soul. Extinction of self that the ideal great self of the universe be all and in all. Therein is peace. But it is at the expense of the extinction of the actual self.

Do not think such interpretation a far-fetched cure. Both Mohammedan and Buddhistic theories are enthroned in us moderns. He who gives up his ideals of virtue and settles back into an accurst contentment, exclaiming, "I will let well enough alone. I will not strive to be the man I thought I would become; my present achievements shall satisfy me," is a Mohammedan modernized. On the other hand, wherever you have a man who out of sheer despondency takes his life you have the Buddhistic philosophy embodied. Poor fellow! The losses and crosses of existence are greater than he can endure. His actual self is all evil in his thought. There is no possibility of peace while his actual self exists. The present is all evil. No peace except I rid myself of myself. A suicide's grave becomes his Nirvana where the ills of life never intrude.

The second problem has found treatment

also. The communist exclaims, "I have solved the question. Get away from all the conflictions incident to civilization and you will have peace. Model society upon apostolic principles. Hold all things in common. Do not let the competitions of trade affect you. Turn your back on the struggle and turmoil. The world is evil. Leave it alone. Save your soul by withdrawing with a few kindred spirits into the wilderness, where the strife comes not to mar your peace."

Thus Quakerism, tho simple and inviting and soul-saving, is not wise. It solves no problem. You can not solve a problem by letting it severely alone.

Such is the genius of Mormonism, a communistic type of living apart from the maddening throng and attaining peace by separating yourself from the ill-adjustments of the great, busy, evil world.

The Socialist is not so exclusive and more heroic. He solves the vexing problem by attacking it. The world is evil, but let us right the wrong by mingling with it and transforming the conditions that produce the conflictions, through legislation, agitation, force.

Let us destroy individualism and make it serve the masses of men that are less favored than itself. Then will peace be universal, for the present false conditions of civilization that make for individual preeminence will be overthrown.

The third problem is likewise solved. God has created all things that exist. He is the responsible author of all ills. Authority is the source of evil. Get rid of authority and you get rid of strife. Peace results. Men can not reach God to dethrone Him, but they can reach the seats of human authority. Therefore, the crowned heads of government are assailed that the common people have a chance to rule themselves, and taste the sweets of liberty untrammeled by laws and governments. Freedom from restraint brings peace, they claim; therefore, deny God, dethrone authority in both divine and human things and all is well.

But in the midst of all the turmoil, and our poor strivings for solution, stands the majestic figure of Jesus Christ, calmly telling us in advance that in the world we shall have tribulation, but in Him peace, and bidding us be of good courage, inasmuch as He has overcome the world. It seems as if the Master of Men foresaw all these attempts at solution, felt the force of all these strivings for peace and wanted to warn us of their inadequacy. The splendid thing about the interpretation of Jesus is that He neither ignores nor endeavors to explain away existing facts and conditions. He is in touch with the God of things as they are; therefore, with things themselves. He never advocated getting rid of either the actual or the ideal selves, but recognized both as God-ordained, and the necessity of struggling from the one to the other.

But, Master, the way is long and rough, the obstacles many, our strivings futile, our strength frail. We fall down and bruise ourselves. We sin each day against God and the best we know.

It was against such a complaint that the full encouragement of His gospel sounded forth, as He maintained that such an unhappy condition was for the glory of God. His forgiveness of our sins, His strength for our weakness, His grace for our ills and sicknesses was sure relief. Jesus saw the battle to be half fought in our recognition of its necessity, and that victory was fully won in struggling to our feet again and pressing toward the goal. So dear to Him was the actual self, however sinful, that He lived for it, died for it; so dear the ideal self of the least among earth's perplexed multitudes that He embodied clearly that ideal in His own divine personality.

What had He to offer upon the second problem? The conflict between ourselves and our surroundings? Did He urge His followers to run away from the world? Did He recommend a war against civilization and individual eminence? His policy was indeed to revolutionize the world, but not to the pulling down of the individual. In fact, the individual was to be safeguarded as the all-important factor in the case, through whom society was to be benefited. He defied the scientific principle, "the survival of the fittest," just as he did many another, and empowered the unfit to survive. Christianity has been repeating the blest prescription ever since, making the unfit, fit; making the fit, fittest. When will we realize that Jesus was God's highest law to man—his very highest mode of expression. And we wouldn't shoot far wide of the mark to see that the personality of man is God's next highest law.

Neither communism nor socialism found favor with Jesus. His attitude toward the world was that it was the best possible for mortals, as are we, to dwell in, and that our sorrows and sicknesses were needed to test our mastery of the situation, conditions in which to assert our latent powers, and manifest our kinship with Him.

I confess that were this world all, the old atheistic contention that God is neither wise nor good has recommendation. But if this world, with its tasks and disciplines, is the preparatory stage—the little primary school necessary to matriculation into the great university, then all is well, and the sad question, who will show us good, is satisfied as the light of His face reveals all things working together for good. I like the thought of the world being the vestibule of the temple beautiful. Paul, with his figures of the darkened glass and our partial knowledge, taught that the glory of the now was as nothing compared to the glory of the by and by. Attitude counts for much. It is, in fact, everything. Christ's standpoint was the grandest possible to mortals. We must regard facts and relations as did He if we would see correctly.

But remember, He wanted men to be as whole and healthy and sane now, while in the vestibule, as by and by in the temple beautiful. He spent as much time in curing men's bodies as He did their souls. The truth is that wherever He went, there the light of God's face shone, which light swept away all abnormality within range of both in spirit and body.

And then about ourselves and God. Did Jesus ever hint even against the divine authority, or urge His followers to have little to do with God? Did He say, as did the Israelites, let not God speak to us lest we die? He rather taught that God must speak to us that we live. And all His precious teaching about the heart of God and His boundless love was to make godliness attractive and God's fatherhood a motive power toward health, manhood and brotherhood in the earth.

Upon Christ's attitude toward the self, the world, and God depends His peace for every troubled heart in all the earth, because it was an attitude on which the light of God's countenance was always shining. Let this mind be in you which was also in Christ Jesus, and the peace of God which passeth understanding, a peace no ill-adjustments can dishearten, that no obstacles can overthrow, shall flood thy soul like a river. The divine sunlight that filled His soul and mantled His face with a glory such as was never on earth, or sea, or sky is God's intention for every erring, stumbling, struggling child of His in all the world.

We said in other places that the Emmanuel movement meant "back to Christ," also to bring Christ forward into our feverish modern existence. Let us also affirm that it also means back to nature, not in the old Socratic sense of being at home in nature, with no higher aspiration, but back to nature as a child of God to receive through nature something of the remedial power the good God has stored up there for His children's needs. Let nature reveal God. It was intended to be an object-lesson of His wise and loving provision, as well as a vast storehouse athrill with remedy for human ills. Our Lord taught that in His reference to the grass, the flowers, and the birds as representative of God's kindly care.

Many a deprest and nervous soul has found marked remedial benefit in drawing in long deep breaths of atmosphere and believing it was His medium of health for heart and soul as well as for lungs and body. Not a few have found relief in a single glass of water, believing that it was charged with the very life vigor of God for bodily ills. Why not? Its simplicity should not make against the virtue of this prescription.

Here, also, Jesus helps us interpret aright. When He gave the bread and wine to His disciples He said this is my body broken, my blood spilled. But it wasn't. It was only bread and wine. But how suggestively He used it. Its virtue was in its suggestion, and that power of suggestion which recently has come to the fore was not only used by the world's greatest psychologist 2,000 years ago, but it is a suggestion as potent to-day as ever, bringing spiritual health to millions of Christians everywhere.

Such is our authority for suggestion to ourselves, also to this commonplace universal life-sustaining air and water, that they are God's specially endowed messengers of health to him who takes them in. And when the air is charged with invigorating sunlight it will not be heretical to believe that the light of God's face is lifted upon you and that you are drinking it in for all health-giving purposes.

Remember it is psychologically orthodox to suggest your desire to the universal life, and if you believe you have received you shall receive because you asked of God. The very atmosphere, commonplace and plentiful, is brimful of curative life vigor, which is instantly enhanced the moment you believe the All Father is using it more effectively to impart divine life than does a Marconi to send thought messages across the seas. Everything is a revelation of God to the soul. Everything a God-created medium to reflect into thy heart peace, and good cheer, to bestow health unto every department of thy nature, and to manifest the light of His face, which will illumine, warm and quicken all thy life.

As upon some mammoth warship of our White Squadron the giant search-light illumines the darkness to reveal the realities concealed there, so the light of God's face flashed upon thy darkened intelligence reveals remedial value in all the great world's commonplace creations to cure thy ills, to enrich thy heart and to help thee realize thy princely heritage as a child of God.

IX

THE EMMANUEL MOVEMENT—I

Wilt thou be made whole?—New Testament Scriptures.

All are bigots who limit the Divine within the boundaries of their present knowledge.
—Margaret Fuller.

All leads up higher,
All shapes out dimly the superior race.
The heir of hopes too fair to turn out false.
. . . . So far the seal
Is put on life. . . . . . .
And a glory mixes with the heaven
And earth, to fill us with regard for man,
Desire to work his proper nature out,
And ascertain his rank and final place;
For these things tend still upward, progress is
The law of life, man is not man as yet.
Nor shall I deem his object served, his end
Attained, his genuine strength put fairly forth
While only here and there a star dispels
The darkness, here and there a towering mind
O'erlooks its prostrate fellows; when the host
Is out at once to the despair of night,
When all mankind alike is perfected,
Equal in full-blown powers, then, not till then,
I say, begins man's general infancy.
—Browning.

IX

THE EMMANUEL MOVEMENT—I

What is it?—How it was begun—Why it was started—The weakening hold of the Church upon the thinking practical masses—The remarkable growth of Christian Science—Diseases attacked and remedied by the Emmanuel movement—Methods of treatment.

THAT is the inspiration of the Emmanuel movement—to make the man whole. It accomplishes this by bringing the whole man under the redeeming power of the Christian religion. An Episcopalian rector and his associate in office conceived the happy idea of making Christian faith do service in the entire psychical and physiological realms. Their studies in psychology convinced them that there was an intimate and powerful relation between the psychic and physical parts in man, and that it was not wise to divide man up into compartments, and say this part is for the priest to prescribe for, as it is psychic, and that part is for the physician to prescribe for, as it is physical, but that man is a unit, an entity;

[243]

that the kind of a mind he has accounts largely for the kind of body he has, and that a healthful spirit, if the man be willing to let the health of the spirit do further service, may become a curative force unto his entire system.

Methinks they also had a conviction on the religious side of the question. They recognized that something had been lost out of Christianity since Jesus asked the infirm man at the pool of Bethesda if he would be made whole, and since Peter commanded the impotent man at the gate of the Temple Beautiful, in the name of Jesus of Nazareth, to rise up and walk. That lost something is that Christianity has a redeeming power for the cure of the body as truly as for the cure of the soul.

Then, further, may they not have felt that the Church was not holding the devotion of men and women as strongly as it should? Preparation for living as a disembodied spirit the other side of the grave is a weak, vague appeal to a man who cares only for living on this side. The proclamation of cure for a spiritual nature that he is not conscious of possessing is wasted energy, compared with the cure of a body whose maladies hold him in painful bondage every hour of the day. We are all of us children still, swayed by the nearest motive rather than by one more remote. And the body looks so much bigger and more important to the majority of mortals than does the spirit that spiritual appeal falls on deaf ears. The Church must present a motive as strong and interesting as does the world, with its appeals of pleasure, of wealth, of sense gratification. Its opportunity is in the assurance of health—present, temporal, bodily health. That strikes hard. It awakens his interest and his response. Yes, but he must become whole in spirit before he can become whole in body. That matters not. He will pay the price, and submit to the spiritualizing treatment if it bear practical, tangible fruitage in the abolishing of pain and achieve his bodily health. Can not the Church, then, meet the need of the hour and possess a more substantial content and meaning for the man of the world?

Then possibly the inaugurators of this precious movement observed that Christian

Science had drawn its constituency by tens of thousands from the very people the established churches, with their prescriptions for death and the life beyond, could not reach; had drawn even from these churches' very membership, and that too on a single issue, and a temporal issue —the cure of the body. They must have noticed, as have we all, that people who for years thundered zealously against evil and its judgments step complacently over into a communion that claims there is no evil nor judgment, that they are errors of mortal mind. And why this going back on all former convictions, all traditional teaching concerning the faith once delivered the saints? Because they or their friends have been healed of bodily infirmity. The question, therefore, must have arisen, can not the churches of established reputation, and high standing in public esteem, of Christian integrity, and missionary aggressiveness, and acknowledged spiritual power, incorporate this feature of applying the Gospel of the Son of God to the restoration of physical health?

Whether consciously actuated by these motives or not, they made the announcement that they would be at the service of any in the parish on Wednesday evenings to talk over the possibility of making the whole man whole. They expected thirty or forty to respond. To their surprize, two hundred and forty attended the first conference. They were soon crowded out of their vestry into the auditorium of the church, and now from five hundred to a thousand people from everywhere gather to hear the simple story of the Gospel that can make over the entire man. In these conferences the causes of disease are expounded, arousement of the dormant psychic nature of the sick person is emphasized, the remedial forces of God's good universe are announced; Christ's cures of numberless bodily ills are proclaimed, His healing power for our present maladies invoked, a spiritual atmosphere created. The troubled, nervous listener experiences the rest and peace to which he was before a stranger, and which he never dreamed of finding.

But such is only the outline of the movement in the large. It is in the individual work that the real test is made. These noble men give themselves untiringly to the individual demanding their help. The morning hours of each day, and the evening hours, too, are given up, a half hour to each person who would be made whole. Organic diseases are not treated: these are handed over to the skilled physician as lying outside of their field. The scientific methods of medical and surgical practitioner are respected. Only those having functional disorders of the nervous system are received. Only those whose maladies have sprung primarily from deranged mental, moral and spiritual conditions are treated. Only those, I say, and yet their name is indeed legion. Dr. McComb quotes a prominent nerve specialist as stating that a generation ago there were 50,000 cases of nervous weakness of one form or another in the United States, and then asserts that now the number has increased to 250,000, due to such prevailing causes as the breakdown of religious faith, the growing artificiality of our social system, the mad rush for wealth, mental idleness and frivolity, use of stimulants and narcotics, lack of self-control from overwork or culpable self-indulgence, all of which produce a neurotic and disordered system. Hence the formidable list of psychic ailments, Dr. McComb continues, to which our American humanity is prone. There is hysteria, which manifests itself in exaggerated emotional displays, such as intense craving for sympathy, or admiration, or in unconscious simulation of various diseases, the fruit of an ill-balanced tho by no means organically diseased brain; hypochondria, or the fixt but groundless belief that a person is suffering from some particular disease; neurasthenia, which covers a vast variety of nerve weaknesses from mild depression to extreme prostration; psychasthenia, in which the patient has a sense of incompleteness, or of the strangeness of things in general, and is the subject of abnormal fears and all kinds of impracticalities; alcoholism, morphinism, cocainism, and drug addictions which end in intellectual and moral degeneration; insomnia, one of the terrible curses of modern life, and an aggravating factor in many diseases; religious melancholy, in which the sufferer imagines himself to have committed the unpardonable sin and that God has abandoned him; fits of anger, of hate, of groundless suspicion which the subject is powerless to conquer, and finally suicidal impulses springing sometimes from deep depression, sometimes from utter disgust of life, sometimes from a sense of shame and despair.

The question is if the Church shall stand by dumb, disinterested and helpless in the midst of suffering as real and intense as that produced by physical causes while men and women are crying out for release from bondage.

How shall the Church proceed? It first of all calls in a physician and thus establishes for the first time a sympathetic and working unity between science and religion. Only such cases are taken in hand as the physician diagnoses have a mental and moral cause and can be cured by mental, moral and spiritual methods.

The first method of cure is "confession," wherein the patient unburdens himself of his worries, confesses his follies and indulgences that go back for years, perhaps, holding him in chains, and binding him to his present diseased condition. Dr. Worcester claims there is large benefit to the sufferer in this opportunity to free his mind to a sympathetic listener. It also opens avenues for insight into the nature of the person's malady, so that curative suggestion can be the easier applied.

We all know the value of a heart-to-heart talk with one who can enter into our grief sympathetically. It relaxes and rests us. The old restrictions become unloosed. We experience a sense of freedom and ease. And if the person to whom we confide the secret of our discontent has the ability to help us out of our misery, our very confidence in him has curative force.

Dr. Worcester also sees in this feature an improvement upon the former plan of pastoral visitation and parish work. Instead of the minister going the rounds of perfunctory visitation, often finding the parishioner not in, or engaged in other things, and if visible in no frame of mind to talk upon the deep things of life, the parishioner now calls on him, if there be a crying need to be satisfied. All ministers know how vast the difference between seeking a person and striving for an opening to get at his difficulty to apply a remedy and the being sought for by that person that religious aid be had.

What may be termed a second method of remedy is the imparting of religious faith. To all persons whose personalities are submerged in immorality, unbelief or the cold empty realizations of the senses, and are therefore deprest and inert, comes the message of hope and faith in God. He is proclaimed as a present, near-by strength, ready to put His infinite power under that life if the person will ask His help. Christ is represented as the giver of rest and peace. The afflicted soul receives the hopefulness offered and for the first time is able to rest and sleep in the new assurance that all is well.

Perhaps a third method of remedy is in remoralizing the life. The emotions have very apparent and violent influence upon the nervous system and the digestive organs and the action of the heart. Tyndall said: "By agreeable emotions nervous currents are liberated which stimulate blood and brain and viscera." Darwin said: "In protracted grief the circulation becomes languid, the face pale, the muscles flaccid, the eyelids droop, the head hangs on the contracted chest. The lips, cheeks and lower jaw all sink downward from their own weight. The whole expression of a man in good spirits is exactly the opposite of the one suffering from sorrow."

If the emotions of fear and worry fill the life, physical derangement results inevitably. Hear Horace Fletcher in his "Menticulture" exclaim, "Worry wastes our bodily energy and paralyzes the digestive and repair functions of the body, painfully wearing out the body itself." How necessary then, since these wise men speak authoritatively, to banish fear, worry and grief and install in their stead the pleasing, cheerful, and joyous emotions, for we will some day learn, God grant soon, that if love and peace pervade the soul, the entire body responds to these health-restorers and a normal state of our functional life results.

Then there is "suggestion" as another

remedial agency. The patient is put into a quiescent state. The will relaxes its striving, mind and body sink down into rest. Complete surrender of the individual to the universal life is realized. The depths of the subconscious self are laid bare, and into these depths, where evil habit is rooted, are put suggestions of health and strength and victory. The patient is made to feel this impartation of the stronger, healthier, hopeful, optimistic self of the person helping him, even of the incoming of the Great Physician's help, and gradually the old evil habits are replaced as consciousness draws upon these strong, true suggestions implanted in the depths below. No small factor in suggestion is the bringing into prominence the man's own latent manhood as a child of God. He is made to believe that his true self, heretofore too weak to assert itself, awaits opportunity to show its ability to dominate the situation.

The new psychology has given us this encouragement. It has revealed an extended resourceful subconscious mind in us all, which as productive soil receives suggestions of whatsoever you choose to impart to its care. Plant there good seed in the nature of health thoughts; give to that fruitful realm ideas of encouragement and assurances of conquest, and it will sprout and grow them, for it is its nature to unquestioningly take just what you impart, and work along the line of the suggestion to victory.

That is why we tell the afflicted one he is a child of God, and that his Father desires him to be healthful, that his life may be well lived.

That also is why we remind him that he has boundless latent resourcefulness just beneath the surface of consciousness that can be drawn on to grow whatever health ideals the person interested in his welfare may impart.

The Emmanuel movement can not be expected to encourage the old theological heresy of total depravity. Nor is its province to emphasize the doctrine of sin, and sin's desert. Its work is remedial throughout. It minimizes depravity. It counteracts the force of sin by lifting as speedily as possible the consciousness above its enslaving power.

It recognizes only the truth and goodness actual in the universal and potential in the individual life. It proclaims the Gospel of redemption, the Gospel of loving kindness and good cheer. It is not even on speaking terms with depravity, sin, failure and condemnation. It emphasizes truth rather than error. Its high calling is to introduce truth —but only truth of a positively remedial character—into the depths of the sin-curst, disease-ridden individual life and set it free. Its sole concern is to make a man whole—splendidly whole mentally, morally, spiritually, bodily.

This desirable actuality is achieved through the ever-present creative imaging faculty in all men. Our human life, which is very plastic and impressionable, is always molded from within. Human bodies are never designless material forms, but fleshly masses of incarnate thought and emotion, solidified into the forms which nature furnishes for our convenience upon this plane of the senses. The expression of this outer material form being always in keeping with the life's mental and emotional content, the only way to eradicate evil is through the individual consciousness. It is a question if evil has any other abiding-place, even tho the theologian can not conceive of it being within unless it is first of all without.

You remember, the old French proverb said, "Paint the devil on the walls and by and by he may appear to you." Better far to paint there hieroglyphics of purity, health, the kind-heartedness of God, the beneficent redeeming face of Christ, and as surely as the day of manly activity follows the rising of the sun will the body respond to these spiritual health thoughts unto all beneficial embodiment.

X

THE EMMANUEL MOVEMENT—II

And they shall call his name Emmanuel, which, being interpreted, is " God with us."—NEW TESTAMENT SCRIPTURES.

And these signs shall follow them that believe. In my name they shall cast out devils; they shall speak with new tongues; they shall lay hands on the sick and they shall recover.—NEW TESTAMENT SCRIPTURES.

The end of life is to be like unto God: and the soul following God will be like unto Him; He being the beginning, middle and end of all things.

—SOCRATES.

Grow soul unto such white estate
That virginal, prayerful art shall be thy breath, thy work,
thy fate.

—SIDNEY LANIER.

THE EMMANUEL MOVEMENT—II

Its "God with us" significance—Its rationality—Its
scientific backing—Its text-books—Some pitiful appeals for help—Christian unity assured—New content
for denominationalism—Revitalizing the Church.

How strangely this latter Scripture falls
upon our ears! Obsolete sentences, indeed,
to ring out from the modern pulpit! The
mention of them is a long swing back into
the past that we were content to leave buried
beyond recall. In our culture, our science,
our rationalizing of Scripture, we thought of
these signs, if we thought of them at all, as
dim and distant sign-posts that could serve
no nobler purpose than to indicate how far
we have progressed in the march of truth.
Since the days of the apostles they have had
no representation except in some insignificant anemic Christian sect or other which,
to be apostolic, has sacrificed forever the possibility of becoming popular. They are, however, the words of the world's Redeemer.
And thrice blest any movement that calls

them from the tomb of human neglect to en-
throne them once more midway, if not in the
forefront, of our faith.

This new Christian movement dares strike
hands with the Master of men, as St. Matthew and St. Mark represent Him, and believe that because God is with us we can cast
out devils, speak with new tongues, heal the
sick.

I regard it providential that this movement
that is to restore to the Church the curative
powers Jesus assured His followers they
should possess was born in a church called
Emmanuel. It is strikingly significant, inasmuch as "God with us" is the inspiration
of the undertaking. "Wilt thou be made
whole?" is its inspiration upon its manward
side; its incentive, its purpose, its field of expression and usefulness. "God with us" is
its inspiration on its Godward side, its
dynamic, its all-necessary encouragement.
Friendly to such Christian ideals, it dares
use all health-restoring aids, the contribu-
tions of psychology, medicine, mental suggestion, Christian Science, faith cure, new
thought and old, appropriating their

strength, discarding their weakness. They all have large modicums of truth as well as considerable mixtures of error. The Emmanuel movement will extract the grain, discard the chaff, and under the leadership of Christ be strong enough to empower the Church for the complete subjugation of the world.

This remarkable movement has no irrationality about it that has yet been detected, tho scrutinized and tested by the keenest minds of the day. Such a famed psychologist as Professor James, of Harvard, gives his approval, stating it is time psychology did something. Dr. Barker, the eminent neurologist of Johns Hopkins University, journeyed to Boston to investigate and returned to Baltimore convinced of its worth, because in harmony with his methods. Dr. Putnam, than whom there is perhaps no more skilled specialist on nervous disorders, has sent numbers of patients to the Emmanuel clinic. Dr. Richard C. Cabot, of the Massachusetts General Hospital, goes on record as saying: "I have examined the complete records of every case handled by Dr. Worcester and his associates, and can say they have accomplished a great deal of good and no harm whatever." I said to Dr. McComb, I came as a sympathetic investigator and not to criticize. His humble reply was, "We welcome criticism. We invite every possible scientific and religious test. We have no desire to carry on this work an hour longer than its legitimacy and worth will warrant." Both patients and critics have probed to the depths of the movement to find rational or moral or religious inconsistencies and failed to detect a single flaw. They have recognized the bronze head and iron loins of the giant, but thought that, like many another health Colossus, his feet might be of clay, but found his feet no weaker than loins and brow.

Their manuals of reference are the voluminous writings of all the great authors on psychology. I asked Dr. Worcester what medical writers he followed for authority and sanction. He put in my hand Dr. Paul Dubois' "Psychic Treatment of Nervous Disorders," professor of neuropathology in the University of Berne, and Dr. Schofield's illuminating work of the British

Medical Society on "The Mental Factor in Medicine." These and the New Testament are some of their handbooks. No wonder their work is distinctively scientific and assuredly Christian. It could be called "scientific Christianity"—and well named—were not Dr. Worcester more humble than presumptuous. With all its scholarly backing and scientific precision and religious consistency, it steps forth open-handed and loving-hearted to bless humanity, without charge or sensational craving for recognition, under the modest caption, "The Emmanuel Movement"—the "God with us" cure for human ills. And the reason it has made so strong an appeal upon Episcopalian and Baptist, Roman Catholic and Jew, is because there is nothing in it that antagonizes their denominational and religious convictions, or ravages their intellectual integrity. The simple, precious doctrine of God with us is a platform on which all men can unite, and it suggests a power that all men can crave.

You remember the despairing sentence the dying infidel wrote with his emaciated hand upon the wall over his head, "God is nowhere." And he fixt his glazed eyes upon it as if to sanction his hopelessness. But his little daughter, just back from Sunday-school, ran in to kiss her dying father on that gloomy afternoon, and read aloud the poor, scrawled, run-together words, exclaiming as she read, "God is now here!" "Oh, papa, God is now here!" It startled him, and his own hand had written it. "If you say so, Nellie, it may be true." That childish heart, filled with the consciousness of God's presence, could not read it otherwise.

Therein is the power of the Emmanuel movement through which men are made whole. With all its correctness of definition, its scientific conception and expression, its splendid psychology, its consistent rationality, it is in both its first and last analysis Emmanuel, the name of Jesus, God with us, God now here.

Better still, it claims that God has been here all the while, for a few hundred centuries or more, and has always been a positive health-giving power, ready to impart His curative Almightiness to every poor, deprest, abnormal mortal that would let the divine sunshine in to flood the chambers of the soul and to cleanse every sin-curst, demon-ridden body into a temple pure and beautiful enough for Himself to dwell in.

Yes, it means back to Christ. But it also means to bring Christ forward into our feverish, fretful modern life. Emerson said, "Hitch your wagon to a star." Dr. Worcester, I presume, would say, "Hitch the stars to your wagon." Let heaven help you drag your load. Clip Christianity's wings, and compel it to walk on two feet. It came down to earth quite a long time ago; keep it down. Make it tread through the dirt and dust of your streets, and all the restricted, unattractive abodes of men, irradiating their experiences and leaving a trail of sunshine everywhere.

Tolstoi hit it right when he said the cause of all our ills is that men have lost their sense of God. That is why we rush at our brother's throat; that is why we struggle and compete, and claw, and cheat, and lose our life more and more with every futile attempt to save it. Yes, and that is the cause of our sorrows, our sicknesses and our despair. We have refused to believe that God was with us and that we were spirits as infinite as is He; and that because spirit with spirit may meet, the very joy of heaven was at our door waiting to be brought up into our consciousness and made the working principle of existence. As Jesus said, "The kingdom of heaven is within you." The declaration is not weakened through the more accurate translation, "The kingdom of heaven is in your midst."

This movement is strikingly in accord with present-day scientific discovery and realization. Into what deep realms of subconsciousness have discoverer and inventor dug to bring up into their consciousness and ours electricity's wonderful displays. If their reliance upon material and mechanical agencies to send thoughts and words through telegraph and telephone were startling, the sending of thoughts and words through the wireless air is more so a hundredfold. Marconi will yet circle the globe with his thought propulsions. Edison assures us that a lone man will in the great

Sahara or in the jungles soon be able to take a little instrument from his pocket and talk with his fellows everywhere. Why? Because God is with us. The world of spirit is more accurately and powerfully communicative than all the mechanical contrivances of earth.

So is this Emmanuel movement vastly more significant than the patient, plodding, remedial work of two earnest churchmen in staid old Boston. Already it has more than the stamp of their genius upon it. The subconsciousness of the human realm is of much more infinite significance than they have probed. God is with us, and the movement may well be said to be in its infancy. No human eye is sufficiently prophetic to see the glorious end.

See, however, what it has done already. It bridges the gulf between the finite and the Infinite, between eternity and time. Yes, I know Christ did it centuries ago, but we haven't lived as tho we thought so. Our churches have been builded upon that bridge. But more to carry us over and up than to bring God over and down. That is why our faith is three parts theory and one part fact. That is why the world, the flesh and the devil have had more allurement for men than the truth of God.

I have forty letters upon my desk, more than half of which offer as introduction to my sympathies the statement that the writer was brought up a Christian, but alas, not such now; that the applicant for cure of ills was once a church attendant, but alas, not that now. Neither church nor ministry is blamed. They got all that was to be had; Christian ideals, splendid doctrines, the location of Jerusalem and the Dead Sea, abstractions on the "blessed Trinity," well-worked-over theology, old or new, what matter which, and some help, doubtless more than they realize. They didn't expect much, and their expectations were met. But the pity of it, the world was stronger than the Church, and there they are, battered diseased hulks, knocking piteously at the doors of the Church for help. In God's name, give. For Christ's sake, help. You are my last resort. Save me or I die.

Thank God, the cry is not in vain. Had we not a positive present remedy to offer, the agony of that cry would break our hearts. Here is one:

I have an almost uncontrollable desire to commit suicide, and would have done so last Saturday night, only I had no means at hand of doing it. To-day I am feeling better, but do not know when the desire may return. I am a widower, thirty-nine years old. One reason I write you is because I am supposed to be a Baptist, but do not attend any church now.

Here is another:

Several years ago I had a severe sunstroke which so shattered my nervous system that I have never recovered my former health, tho I have spent a fortune endeavoring to do so. I am in business, but unable to meet my expenses, and with creditors pressing me. With bankruptcy staring me in the face and a deplorable mental condition, I have grave fears that I will lose my reason and do some desperate act. It appears to me that I haven't a friend on earth. Oh, sir, help me to escape from this terrible bondage of melancholia and thus confer an everlasting favor upon me, and God will surely bless you for doing so. Earnestly praying you will consider my unfortunate circumstances and heed my appeal, etc.

Here is a third, every word of which you must bear with me while I read:

Seeing an article describing your desire to treat certain diseases, alcoholism being one of them, with mental suggestion and by surrounding the patient with uplifting thoughts, I have taken the liberty of writing you regarding the drug habit, asking your help for myself and friend as a last resort. We are both young men, twenty-two years old, and are addicted to the use of morphine. If you could help us you would earn our everlasting gratitude and affection. It may seem forward and bold to have a total stranger write to you, but if you could only know the torture and suffering that one addicted to this debasing habit goes through you would not wonder at my boldness in writing you. It is as a drowning man grasping at a straw. If you could see your way clear to help us we would never be able to repay the obligation, etc.

And what of him who writes his wife is in a sanatorium with religious dementia, brought on through the loss of "our little home through a building and loan association. And, oh, sir, our little girl of three years cries so bitterly, and calls so loudly for her mother. Take pity on a sorrowing husband and father."

We call this a movement for the healing of the body. It could be more appropriately called a movement for the uplifting of the soul unto its divine and infinite possibilities of power to live in a clean, newly furnished house, with all modern improvements; yes, and ancient improvements, too, and where the man can enjoy all the comforts of home.

It is simply a movement to help the Church embrace a hitherto neglected field of usefulness; a divine call for the Church to assure men that God is with us for the cure of the body, as well as for the cure of the soul. To tell men that, however hard their circumstances without and their evil habits within, they can become absolute masters of their fate.

Then how splendidly it makes for that Christian unity the Master had in mind when He said: "That they may all be one, Father, as I am in thee and thou in me." God with us, always makes for unity. No movement or church called Emmanuel has a. right to be altogether and forever sectarian. Its field is in the open. Its sphere of usefulness is everywhere this side the stars. Ask the dear man who feels called to safeguard his creed and the precious dogmas of the denomination to yield a point upon a single doctrinal question, tho that traditional statement for vital righteousness is straw and stubble, and he imagines himself a Luther, exclaiming: "I can not; truly I can not. Here I stand, God helping me,

[273]

I can do no more." But put a new love into his heart for humanity, impart an enthusiasm for a great righteous cause, and in spite of himself he becomes, in sympathy at least, a member of the Church universal, and God's angels pass in and out, perhaps for the first time, across the threshold of his life.

Then how needed is some such awakening to revitalize the Church. It is becoming the popular thing to give up the midweek devotional meeting for testimony praise and prayer. Presbyterian, Congregationalist, Baptist are following each year more and more this popular trend. If the meeting be continued it is quite a formal thing. A few hymns sung, often at a poor, dying rate, a chapter of Scripture, a prayer or two and a ministerial address. Such is not universal. There are multitudinous exceptions to this Dead March in Saul procedure. But it is prevalent. But I notice the Church in Boston where this movement was inaugurated has a devotional service for the first time in its history, and for a year or more each week ministers devotionally to between 500 and 800 souls. Then I have observed both in Boston and New York that the Christian Science churches congregate in a single church larger numbers still each Wednesday night to praise God and Mother Eddy for their deliverance from the errors of mortal mind.

In saying all this it is not meant to be implied that the churches of our faith are not doing much splendid work for God and man. They are. Without them the kingdom could not have become the realistic fact it is. Only eternity will be opportunity enough to reveal the far-reaching extent of their faith and good works. They are the lights set on a hill that have illumined the dark places of the earth, dissipated death's gloom, and guided countless multitudes into a joyful eternity. They are the salt that hath by no means lost its savor to make life pure, transform character, reorganize society. All we require further is that they send their illuminating, preserving power into the whole man to make him whole. All we demand is that they incorporate the "God with us" doctrine unto the casting out of demons; the demons of deranged personality, of neurotic and disordered temperament, of miserable foreboding that drives out sleep and peace, tying up the man in a body with innumerable diseases and through which no health-producing spirit flows.

And how shall these diseases be cured? By laying hands on the sick is the scriptural advice, hands of faith, of prayer, of health-producing thought, of spiritual power. Physical contact is but one of the many mediums of approach and helpless if there be no spiritual power behind.

The world was a very small, contracted, hand-to-hand place in those old apostolic days. The enlargements of God have come in. Expansions incredible until they appeared have arrived. Neither remedial thought nor healing spirit need fleshly touch to conduct them to their desired end. God is with us in greater power than in the Galilean days. Mechanicalism, naturalism recede as the flood-tides of spirit rise, as did John the Baptist in the presence of the Christ. Repentance is good; but grace and truth are better. Wires and hands useful, at certain stages of development indispensable; but the wireless atmosphere and the spirit's touch are more intelligent and more universal means of communication.

To say all this is to affirm that creation waits upon recreation; the first birth upon the second; sense perception upon faith, sight upon insight, nature upon spirit. Life's best day is when we realize God's near power for many more of our human ills than the established creeds enumerate. As the Scriptures put it: "My God shall supply all your needs according to His riches in glory by Christ Jesus."

XI

THE EMMANUEL MOVEMENT AND CHRISTIAN SCIENCE

But they that wait upon the Lord shall renew their strength; they shall mount up with wings as eagles; they shall run and not be weary; and they shall walk and not faint.—OLD TESTAMENT SCRIPTURES.

Thinketh no evil.—NEW TESTAMENT SCRIPTURES.

The evil is null, is naught, is silence implying sound—
On the earth the broken arcs; in the heaven a perfect round.
—BROWNING.

Man is permitted much
To scan and learn
In nature's frame
Till he well-nigh can tame
Brute mischiefs, and can touch
Invisible things, and turn
All worrying ills to purposes of good.
—JOHN HENRY NEWMAN.

No human eyes thy face may see;
No human thought thy form may know;
But all creation dwells in thee,
And thy great life through all doth flow.
—THOMAS WENTWORTH HIGGINSON.

XI

THE EMMANUEL MOVEMENT AND CHRISTIAN SCIENCE

A contrast—Criticism of Christian Science—Appreciation of Christian Science — Citations from ''Science and Health''—The one point in common with the Emmanuel movement—The many points of difference—Physicians as necessary powers of help, and as unnecessary nuisances—The Christian Science self-centered standard of healing in contrast with Christ's unselfish ideals— How Christian Science and the Emmanuel movement regard the Scriptures—Mrs. Eddy's hoped-for philanthropy—How Christian Science and the Emmanuel movement try to satisfy the world's need.

In this discussion of Christian Science in contrast with the Emmanuel movement, I will impose upon myself two limitations. First, I will not speak upon its metaphysical, its theoretical side. I presume the reason critics give it such inhospitable treatment is because its metaphysics seems preposterously wrong according to all rational, psychological and theological standards as to the constituency of God, man, nature, and the world. It is its practical side that interests

[281]

me most—altogether, in fact, so far as our present meditation is concerned.

The second limitation is that I approach Christian Science as an investigator. I can not be as sympathetic, therefore, as the disciples of Christian Science would desire, for mine is an outside view, rather than an inside revelation. Were I on the inside of the supposed charmed sphere, my approach would not be a questioning one. But being an outsider, you must expect this questioning attitude, and be prepared for all it implies. You may be disappointed then, but you will not be grieved, for you have no right to expect compliance with your teachings or support of your organization.

Another class of persons will also be disappointed because I am not more critical in scrutiny, and do not make sweeping denunciation. It is a native trait to be intolerant. Tolerance is an acquired virtue, fruitage of a balanced mind, a just disposition, a loving heart, or a genial spirit. Sometimes the more tenaciously we hold a doctrine the more distinctively critical are we of all outside of it. Such persons can not bear to hear a seemingly contrary truth mentioned except to denounce it. All such need to learn a fundamental fact; namely, that there are more things in heaven and earth than those dreamed of in their philosophy. Truth is such a big thing, while all approaches to it are such little introductory avenues. I, for one, can not approach so serious a question in the spirit of destructive criticism. It is always easier to destroy than to create. More damage can be done in an hour by a tearer-down than can be repaired in a year by one who would build up. Then, again, you are disarmed in getting at facts. I can not wield such a sledge-hammer weapon. I am too anxious to get at the other fellow's viewpoint. Believe me, therefore, to be an impartial investigator, and tho you do not agree with my conclusions, you will respect my fairness.

A body of people who pick up a truth the Christian Church drops, and push it fearlessly and helpfully, have a right to receive both fairness and tolerance of treatment. That truth is that there is divine power in the universe that can be applied to diseased bodies with remedial and curative effect. I thank Christian Science for that truth. And I thank all others who have in less prominent ways wielded it. It is not original with Christian Science, except in the form under which it is presented. Both Roman Catholic and Protestant churches have applied that remedial truth through the centuries. And there was once a Galilean who was quite an adept at that sort of thing. But it had not before been made a separate issue, and raised to supreme place, and builded into an institution.

But, you exclaim, how can God bless with curative power lives whose standards are irrational, definitions incorrect, methods unscientific and absurd? How often have I asked that very question of this same irrational, unscientific, strikingly peculiar, but withal Christian cult. I have asked it when I have read the sentences by which the book "Science and Health" is introduced to our confidence, in which the claim to divine inspiration is consciously implied, and in which I am told that "No human pen or tongue taught me the science contained in this book,

and neither tongue nor pen can ever overthrow it. This book may be distorted by shallow criticism, or by careless or mischievous
students, and its ideas may be forced into
wrong channels, but science and truth therein
will remain forever to be discerned and demonstrated."

I again asked the question when I visited
their public temples and saw it cut into the
solid stone, on one side the word of our Lord
or one of His apostles, and by its side an
explanatory word of Mrs. Eddy, both of
equal authority; in fact, her word more
necessary and authoritative than the word of
Christ, else it would not have been there in
imperishable setting.

I asked that question when my eye fell upon
this paragraph wherein Mrs. Eddy's book is
clothed in the very words once written of the
word of God, tho sadly perverted and misap-
plied, "Then will a voice from harmony cry,
Go take the little book. Take it and eat it up,
and it shall make thy belly bitter, but it shall
be in thy mouth sweet as honey. Mortal, obey
the heavenly evangel. Take up Divine Science.
Read it from beginning to end. Study it.

Ponder it. It will be indeed sweet at its first taste when it heals you; but murmur not over Truth, if you find its digestion bitter.''

I again asked that question when I read this irrational statement: ''Gender is a quality, a characteristic of mind not matter.''

Also when reading this astounding, shameless confession: ''In the early years of Christian Science, among my many thousands of students few were wealthy. Now Christian Scientists are not indigent and their comfortable fortunes are acquired by healing mankind morally, physically, spiritually.''

Did Christ exchange His gifts of healing for gold? Did He boast of, or encourage, financial possession in His followers? But He did tell one who would follow Him to ''go and sell all he had and give to the poor.'' The good cheer and health of the Gospel was His fee, and all are urged to come and possess God's best life without money and without price.

Quite a glaring difference between that beneficent missionary endeavor whose inspiration is to give, give, and the Christian Science demand to get, get. So I too, not only when contemplating Christian Science's glaring inconsistencies and false standards, but also when reflecting upon those statements that savor of mental and religious aberration, have asked how can God bless such absurd teachings. But the more I have thought about it all the more have I recalled the loving kindness of God, who never confines His blessings to the deserving only, nor to the intellectually consistent, but lets His rain fall alike upon the just and unjust. Then have I recalled that sincerity is the saving grace, at least, when there is a crying need to be satisfied however irrational the thinking back of it.

Out of the heart are the issues of life. It is not what sloughs off from the top of a man's head that counts. With God the primary thing is human need, not what the needy one thinks cosmologically, astronomically or theologically. It is not that God blesses erroneous mentality, but in spite of it. I suspect that by and by we will be quite shaken up to find out how little God cares about viewpoints and intellectual attitudes and scientific approaches, and theological treatises and catechisms and creeds. The truth of the matter is that God is so much more interested in us than we are in Him, even than we are in ourselves, and that He is so exceedingly anxious to put His abundant eternal life into us, that He is quick to take advantage of any little opening to send into the human spirit His exceeding largeness and uplift. I think Christ's comparison of faith to a grain of mustard-seed has some such significance. Seeing all this is to realize that men are blest of God, not because of what they know, but of what they need.

That does not mean that the Omniscient One puts a premium on ignorance either. Nor is it to affirm that Christian Science is right or wrong upon its intellectual side. It's a question whether rightness or wrongness applies to intellectuality anyway. Be that as it may, Christian Science has gotten hold of a truth about divine healing that is backed by numberless trustworthy testimonies. And it not only spells health for the body but exhilaration of spirit also, and happiness of heart, and reliance on the Bible and devotion to God.

I would designate Christian Science as a branching off from Christianity on a single line unto an important work, and carrying some of Christianity's charm with it, while I would designate the Emmanuel movement as a broadening out of Christianity to take in a new and long-neglected field, and cultivating it with good seed.

To change the figure. It has always seemed to me that Christian Science was trying to play a symphony on one string, and succeeding tolerably well. It's amazing how much music you can get out of one string. But I prefer at least four to my violin. And as for symphonies, an entire orchestra doesn't come in amiss. They get, however, a good deal of melody out of the unique situation—beautiful, soul-soothing melody— in which there is never a discord. But to me continuous melody gets monotonous after a while. I must say I prefer harmony, with its varied tones, its multiple chord formations, in which many a discord is, but all blended, both evenly and symmetrically, with the many compounded parts. That comes nearer imitating the music of the spheres.

But there is this one point in common between Christian Science and the Emmanuel movement, that both desire to remedy bodily ills. True, they no sooner join issue than they disagree and, like some uncongenial husband and wife, separate. The point of separation is the nature of curable and incurable malady. The Emmanuel movement exclaims only "functional disorders of the nervous system" can enter our clinic. Christian Science exclaims "functional and organic diseases, too," can have our cure. Here is where Christian Science shows splendid tho not commendable daring. No disease under heaven feases it. Its daring is admirable. Its consciousness of power superb. Its presumption almost contagious, if not quite. I should say its consciousness of limitless power was its weak point. But wouldn't its consciousness of limited power be a weaker? It seems so, surely, even to its undoing. Therefore, it pushes ahead with all assurance, even tho it, at times, fails to make good. It, however, works successfully enough times—and, they claim, in the most hopeless kinds of organic diseases—to justify existence. This only point of similarity then becomes the first point of difference.

A second point of contrast is in its attitude toward the powers that be. The Emmanuel movement claims that the powers that be are ordained of God, with especial reference to medical and surgical powers. Christian Science claims that the powers that be are no powers at all. I admit to being old-fashioned enough to claim that physicians are among the greatest benefactors of humanity. President Eliot, of Harvard, goes me one better, exclaiming, "the very greatest." Christian Science would not even be polite enough to call them necessary nuisances in its firm belief, against the intelligence of the ages, that they are both nuisances and unnecessary. But of what account is the intelligence of the ages save to emphasize admirably the existence of the errors of mortal mind?

Then Christian Science denies nature. The Emmanuel movement doesn't need to. Christian Science, possibly, is afraid that if it admits nature's existence it may fall under its charm. The Emmanuel movement does not have to deny nature, either to get away from its charm or to dominate it. I presume, however, the Christian Scientist, like many other idealists, enjoys idealization. I plead guilty to being something of an idealist myself. I have said more than once that time was nothing, that eternity was all; that time was only the one little segment of the infinite circle, revealed and adapted to us, while the other ninety-nine parts were hidden; therefore, being an adaptation of eternity, time had no reality other than eternal reality. But, alas, to us little-time mortals unto whom and for whom it has been adapted, it has reality! The changing seasons, the flying years emphasize it; while from an eternal standpoint it has none.

You see, it is the old philosophic conception that started way back in the Vedas and Upanishads of India; then passed over into Plato, then forward to Kant; namely, that the noumenal world is all and the phenomenal world nothing. But the phenomenal world has to be reckoned with. It does not evaporate readily enough to suit the practical man. So the practical man grapples with it instead of denying its existence. Therein is both the strength and weakness of Christian Science in its tremendous irrational denials.

Rationally there is no possible justification for its strange procedure. Sir Oliver Lodge exclaims: "Denial of all sides of a problem but one is the weakness and delusion of Christian Science. They hold one side of truth, and in so narrow and insecure a fashion that in self-defense they think it safest simply to deny the existence of all other sides." No rational justification, we say. But therapeutically redemptive nevertheless. Out Platoing Plato and out Berkeleying Berkeley, our two most extreme idealists, but so psychologically intensive on a single point that most desirable results are attained. In their case the end justifies the means they claim, so what matters it tho the intellectual and religious world look on in amazement. Tho their great denials of what all normal mortals call reality is their weakness and their strength, their true strength is in their power to affirm a universal health principle which is theirs, also ours for the asking.

Everything follows from this—repose, for instance. A French proverb says, "When a man does not find repose in himself, it is in vain for him to seek it elsewhere." The Christian Scientist is the most reposeful mortal on the face of the earth. Why not so? Everything he dislikes he denies—inconveniences, annoyances, temptations, sin, pain and sickness. Those grand old lines come to my mind:

> Not in the clamor of the crowded street,
> Not in the shouts and plaudits of the throng,
> But in ourselves are triumph and defeat.

Thus, also, mastery is theirs, without the struggle of conquest. Napoleon said: "I have only one counsel for you—be master." True, Napoleonic mastery was quite a different thing from Christian Science mastery. But both mastery notwithstanding. Claudius exclaimed, "No man is free who is not master of himself."

The Christian Scientist admirably embodies the dictum of grand old Edmund Spenser in his "Faerie Queene," who said—

> It is the mind that maketh good or ill,
> That maketh wretch or happy, rich or poor.

Christian Science is the most prolific creator of fairy queens in existence, and all living in fairy palaces. No small achievement, I assure you, to build a fairy palace in the midst of this sordid old earth. The Christian Scientist of all men has a right to affirm that the air castle is the only real castle in all the world. Thus the Christian Scientist constructs for himself an ethereal world where esthetic tendencies prevail.

The Emmanuel movement has not found the world so ideal that its actual existence must be denied in order that it may be readily dealt with; nor, on the other hand, has it found the world too substantially big and evil to be benefited by its remedial force. It sees the world to be an actual affair all alive with possibilities of evil and good, of disease and health, ever awaiting our human interest and packed full of opportunity for work and achievement.

Just another contrast: Christian Science claims the Scriptures to be a sealed book, a locked treasure-house until it applies the key. The Emmanuel movement proceeds upon the conviction that the Scriptures are so open and simple and illuminating for all devotional purposes that human keys are more likely to turn the wrong way, and lock instead of open. Then there is that precious Lord's Prayer. We thought it sufficiently self-revealing as it fell from Jesus' lips. But it seems its language needs to be improved; its clear, crisp, simple thought interpreted in other style and speech.

And yet this text from Isaiah, one of the most beautiful, is very appropriate to the Christian Science faith. It waits upon the Lord to renew its strength, and mounts as on wings of eagles. Its aspirational side is to me delightful to contemplate. It soars clear up into the sunlit realm of the Divine Mind, as does the eagle into the eye of the sun. It basks in the light of God's face. No small achievement. Would that the staid old conservative churches of Christendom had such superb aspirational powers.

Christian Science also runs and is not weary, walks and is not faint. It is in constant touch with its source of strength. But while the Emmanuel movement is also aspirational, it may be said to be strongest upon its extensional side. This illustration may serve to show what I mean. A few months ago the founder of Christian Science was heralded as giving a million dollars to the poor. "Splendid!" cried the world. "It is at last making a disinterested contribution to humanity. Mrs. Eddy is at last going to yield up a million of her psychic gains to found a charity for the poor. Mrs. Eddy's name will become linked with such public benefactors as Rockefeller, Carnegie and Mrs. Sage." But, alas! for the poor indeed, but only for such of them as would study Christian Science. That is what I mean by saying it is more aspirational than extensional. It runs out into the world to bend the world to itself. On the other hand, the Emmanuel movement, which is the Church at work, runs forth into the world to cure its ills with higher incentive than to bend it to itself, whatever denominational name that self be known by.

Christian Science may be likened to a tree —a tall, graceful palm, if you choose— springing up out of the arid, sandy plain of our social and commercial life. It is strikingly branchless, but has luxuriant foliage at the top, and under its kindly shade the wearied and sick find refreshment and rest. The Emmanuel movement, on the other hand, has no independence to boast of. It is simply a new shoot, carefully grafted into the grand old fruit-bearing denominational trees, to help them bear fruit so luscious and tempting that the world is eager to pluck and eat for its daily nourishment and life.

XII

THE EMMANUEL MOVEMENT AND JESUS CHRIST

The prayer of faith shall save the sick, and the Lord shall raise him up, and, if he have committed sins, they shall be forgiven him. Confess your faults one to another, and pray one for another that ye may be healed. The effectual fervent prayer of a righteous man availeth much.—NEW TESTAMENT SCRIPTURES.

Worship's deeper meaning lies
In mercy, and not sacrifice.
Not proud humilities of sense
And posturing of penitence,
But love's enforced obedience.

.   .   .   .

Christ dwells not afar,
But here amidst the poor and blind,
The bound and suffering of our kind;
In works we do, in prayers we pray,
Life of our life He lives to-day.

—WHITTIER.

Was some one asking to see the soul?
See your own shape and countenance.

—WALT WHITMAN.

XII

THE EMMANUEL MOVEMENT AND JESUS CHRIST

Christ's attitude toward the healing of the body—The attitude of Peter, Paul and James—Why a lost art?—Despising the body—Rise of monasticism—A corrupt Church—Epicureanism and stoicism—Kantianism —Back to Christ—Restricting and enlarging the purpose of the Church—The testimony of John Wesley upon value of religious therapeutics—A nurse's letter in behalf of an Emmanuel movement cure of excessive alcoholism—The patient's tribute to the redemptive power of Christ after five months of abstinence—Our deplorable ecclesiastical situation—Right kind of Church extension.

It is astonishing how much the Scriptures say of the cure of the body, all of which is hidden to the reader until he looks for it, else has his attention called thereto. These cures are like nuggets of gold and silver lying upon the surface, but unobserved to all passing that way with gaze fixt upon the sky. The synoptic Gospels contain a revelation along this line, marvelous to behold. I ran through one of these, the Gospel of St. Matthew, and found hundreds of cases, all

flashing intelligence into the mind in behalf
of Christ's eagerness to make sick people
well, like diamond points scintillating light.

The features of this revelation were more
astonishing than the revelation itself. In
few cases is the cure of the soul included by
any statement made, existing therefore only
in inference, the cure of the body being primary and often the sole concern. Many are
healed on another's faith, as in the case of
the Centurion's servant, the daughter of
the Canaanitish woman, the man whose son
was a lunatic, and the man sick of the palsy.
In only one case of these hundreds does the
Master forgive sins first.

When he sends out His twelve disciples
His charge to them reads thus: He gave
them power over unclean spirits to cast them
out, to heal all manner of sicknesses and all
manner of diseases. And when He bids them
preach that the kingdom of heaven is at
hand he continues: "Heal the sick, cleanse
the lepers, cast out devils." When John
sends his messengers from the prison to determine if he were the Messiah, He exclaims:
"Tell John what ye see and hear; the blind

receive their sight, the lame walk, lepers are cleansed, the deaf hear, the poor have the Gospel preached to them." He thus puts the healing of the body in the very forefront of His ministry, and He bids His disciples put it in the very forefront of theirs, making it their first concern. He, moreover, shows such anxiety to banish disease that He does not pause to require faith on the sufferer's part. Nor does He seem to transmit His healing power through a healthy mind and a cleansed soul. In many cases there is no way of telling how many He heals involuntarily. In the case of the diseased woman the hem of His garment is touched. On another occasion we read, they brought all that were diseased that they might touch the hem of His garment, and as many as touched were made whole.

What is the summing up of it all, if not that the tides of spiritual power were always coursing through Jesus, charging with healing force even His garments.

After Christ's departure from the earth the cure of the body becomes incidental to the cure of souls. The disciples are so intent upon spreading the kingdom that they have more important things to attend to, in proclaiming Him the Son of God, His resurrection from the dead, the forgiveness of sins in His name, the establishing of the Christian Church.

But the divine power for the cure of disease is still present. Peter heals the lame man at the gate of the temple. Later, they bring their sick and lay them by the roadside that His shadow fall upon them.

Paul wrought cures both at Lystra and Ephesus. He at Lystra enabled the man crippled from his mother's womb to walk and leap. At Ephesus the enthusiasm ran so high that they brought aprons and handkerchiefs to be charged with his healing power. They then placed these upon the sick, and the diseases, we read, departed from them and the evil spirits went out of them.

Then comes James into prominence, with his gospel of works. Of all men the practical one, simple, concise, epigrammatic, broad, humanitarian. "Be ye a doer of the Word." "Faith without works is dead"; "Guard your tongue, it is a fire, a world of iniquity";

"Pure and undefiled religion is this, to visit the widows and the fatherless in their affliction and to keep himself unspotted from the world." And yet he can not close his epistle without exclaiming: "Is there any sick among you, call in the elders of the Church, the prayer of faith shall save the sick. Confess your faults, pray one for another, that ye may be healed." It looks as tho this advice were given at the close of his epistle just because he is so broad and humanitarian.

There can be no question but that our Lord intended the ministry of healing to continue, and that it was a matter of grave importance to Him that it should.

Why, then, has this ministry become a lost art? Because we are still hampered by medieval thought regarding the body. That thought is that the body is the chief hindrance to the soul's progress.

We know what the Dark Ages meant to the Church. They came near killing it out. The corruptions of the age came in. The world and the sensuous realizations of the body overthrew spiritual zeal. The Church's ideals fell. Her standards trailed in the dust.

Her priesthood became licentious. Her bishops and archbishops debauched. A righteous remnant came out and founded monastic orders. The monastery saved the Church from dissolution, and kept religion pure from worldly and sensuous taint. But at great cost. Asceticism ruled. Their concern was to save the soul. The body is the great curse. In it all evil dwells. It possesses no good. Therefore, crucify it. Beat it with stripes. Deny its demands. Starve out its strength. Fast and pray. Through poverty, starvation, scourging and all conceivable denial it must be kept under. It and the world were wholly bad. Get away from both and save the soul. It was a strenuous attempt to live the simple life.

Their inspiration was taken, possibly, from Christ's words: "If thy hand offend thee, cut it off; if thine eye offend thee, pluck it out." For, said Jesus, it were better to enter into the eternal life maimed physically than to retain your physical completion and lose it. True. "For what is a man profited to gain the world and lose himself."

Then we know how perilous is reliance

upon the gratification of the senses. Of course, life is restricted sadly when even one of these avenues of expression is blocked. The blind man, the deaf man are pitiful to behold. We thank God we have five unimpeded ways of approaching the world,' five precious means of receiving the beauty, the melody, the fragrance, the sweetness and the substance of nature. But poor, indeed, is he who has no soul faculty for seeing the sights on the other side the horizon. To be pitied, he who hears no music of the spheres. Of all men, miserable, if he has no susceptibility for God.

So thought those medievals who through asceticism led anemic lives in monastic cells. Therefore, it was a choice between bodily vigor and spirituality.

Then there was another line—a philosophic, along which the necessity for asceticism came in. Epicureanism is as prevalent to-day as it was two hundred years before Christ. Nothing is worth while but pleasure is its cry. "Let us eat, drink and be merry; for to-day we live and to-morrow we die," is its inspiration. We, like all the followers of Epicurus, have degenerated into desire for quantity and intensity of pleasure. ` Let life run riot. Let luxury, extravagance, sensuous enjoyment and dissipation fill out the day. That is and was epicureanism at its worst. Then sprang up stoicism, and Zeno, Seneca, and Marcus Aurelius became the saviors of their day. "Man must have no passions at all." "Emotion is a disease and not to be tolerated for a moment." "Health of soul recognizes neither passion nor emotion." "Pleasure is transitory, tiresome, sickly; it hardly outlives the tasting of it." Seneca exclaims: "I am seeking what is good for man, not for his body." Rigor, austerity, became their chief concern. If the countenance is ever illumined it must be a stolid smile that lights up the face. Neither sorrow nor joy must be allowed to enter the heart. Perpetual calm must become its feast. Pity is weakness. Compassion and sympathy are death. Such is stoicism. A violent rebound from all body gratifications. And there is a deal of religious stoicism in existence now.

Then there is Kantianism. We can never

repay our indebtedness to the German, Immanuel Kant, for his rigorous ideals of duty. But his splendid ''Categorical Imperative'' spells out only half the truth. It is not life. It is only theory about life at its severest, rather than at its best. Not duty for duty's sake altogether. Life is broader and richer than duty can spell out. Pleasure must be reckoned with. Happiness must have representation. Morality—cold, commanding and unyielding—must not bend humanity wholly to itself. Rather must it bend itself to humanity. Life is bigger than all else. Value is the only reality that shall dominate it. And value takes in duty, morality, pleasure, happiness, and all else that it can use to demonstrate its worth.

And where do we find ourselves standing to-day? If epicureanism be not allowed to give us the cue to living, neither shall stoicism. If hedonism, the call of pleasure must not enslave us, neither shall intuitionism, the call of conscience and duty. If worldliness and sensuousness be not permitted to claim the throne, neither shall the asceticism of medieval or modern times.

Man, because he is God's best creation, must be a child of freedom. He shall know the truth and the truth shall make him free.

So the place of emphasis has shifted. It is not to live as tho there were no world to enlist your sympathy. But to be in the world molding it, purifying it, using it for your good. Nor is it to live as tho you were a disembodied soul. But to make the body fit habitation for the soul. It is not that either world or body are so bad that you, to be spiritual, ignore them. But it is that both exist that you may master them. Use them freely, honorably; but don't let them use you. Go down into the world hourly, if you choose, but down because you live above the world. Live in the body joyously, because you live in the spirit and can not, therefore, inhabit the body on other terms.

The Emmanuel movement is a very timely help to this desired end. It recognizes life in the body and the world, as did Jesus of Nazareth centuries ago, and grapples with the situation to make the man master of his fate. It sees the world to be a beautiful rather than a dreadful place to dwell in. It

views the body as comely and plastic, with
possibilities to become a veritable temple
beautiful when that skilled artist, the spirit,
hath chiseled all its graces into it; even made
it a temple fitted to be the abiding-place of
the Holy Ghost.

Do I seem to be introducing into life a new
and unfamiliar force? Rather an old ac-
credited power, a power as old as Nazareth;
that stood the test of Calvary; that rose
triumphant from the tomb, and ours, by virtue of our faith in the Son of God.

A Christian force in very truth, but only
new and unfamiliar to the soul unacquainted
with Jesus Christ. The most devout of the
centuries have not been altogether strangers
to this remedial truth. Hear that royal soul
John Wesley, the founder of Methodism, exclaim: "I earnestly advise every one, together
with all his other medicines, to use that medicine of medicines, prayer. Where is the cure
for either lingering or impetuous passions
that either furiously overturn this house of
earth, or saps the foundations of health and
life by sure approaches. The whole *materia
medica* is of no avail in this case. What can

cure it but the peace of God. No other medicine under heaven. What but the love of God, that sovereign balm for the body as well as the mind. The passions have a greater influence on health than most people are aware of. All violent and sudden passions dispose to or actually throw people into acute diseases. The slow and lasting passions, such as grief and hopeless love, brings on chronic diseases. Till the passion which caused the disease is calmed medicine is applied in vain. The love of God, as it is the sovereign remedy of all miseries, so in particular it effectually prevents all the bodily disorders the passions introduce by keeping the passions themselves within due bounds. And by the unspeakable joy and perfect calm, security and tranquillity it gives the mind, it becomes the most powerful of all means of health and long life.''

I asked one of my church officials what he thought of this new movement. His answer rebuked me, as he exclaimed, ''What is there new about it?'' ''Nothing new,'' said I. ''Only the old Gospel under a new name, stepping forth to inhabit a new sphere of usefulness, and to make conquests there.''

Just a further question: Does the Emmanuel movement restrict or enlarge the purpose of the Church? Well, that depends upon what the purpose of your church may be. If the Church exists only to prepare men for eternity, it restricts its purpose; for it turns the Church's attention to the earth and the concerns of time. It does not help men to be carried to the skies on flowery beds of ease, but it does help them to fight their battles here upon the earth and live nobly, and win out even before the end of the strife. It has no interest in enabling a man to read his title clear to mansions there, but it does show him how his title can be searched and found valid here in the homes of men, the haunts of vice, the dust-filled avenues of earth.

Then again, if your church exists to perpetuate ecclesiastical formality, denominational regularity, creedal and doctrinal substantiality, the Emmanuel movement calls a sorry halt upon your dry-as-dust endeavors; for it has no higher ambition than to make some poor human creature whole.

You remember the story of the two boys who, upon a sultry summer Sunday afternoon, were learning their catechism. One said to the other, "How far have you got?" "I'm beyond redemption," was the facetious answer. "You are?" exclaimed the questioner. "My! I'm in the middle of original sin." The Emmanuel movement knows nothing about and cares less for either original sin, or any such theoretical redemption. It does, however, occupy itself with the ravages of sin. It does carry to the lowliest, most outcast, most despairing soul upon the earth a full, rich every-day redemption.

It has been said that this full, rich, every-day redemption that the Emmanuel movement achieves is more physical than spiritual. The objection has been hurled in our faces that this movement emphasizes human completeness rather than the completeness that is in Christ. In reply to all this I would quote the written word of one cured of excessive alcoholism. But that we may realize how bad this case was I would first of all cite the words of the nurse in attendance upon the case in question:

I was recently nurse, during days of delirium, to a man who has for many years been fighting against periodical attacks of severe alcoholism. So-called "cures," sanatoriums and doctors were unsuccessful. In despair we applied to Dr. MacDonald for possible help through the Emmanuel movement, and the doctor consented to take him. There were five conferences, extending over nine days, and he has not touched a drop since the first.

That day I left him alone for several hours, when he triumphantly showed me a full bottle of whisky accidentally discovered where I had secreted it, and which he had abstained from drinking, altho sorely tempted.

After the second conference, on seeing a big whisky sign, telling a certain brand is "best," he responded mentally, "That's a lie; there is no good in it," reiterating it whenever the haunting thought recurred to him. After the third conference he went and paid his saloon bills, informing his old associates they would never see him again and refusing to touch a drop, in spite of laughter and ridicule.

He is following the Emmanuel teachings, full of hope for the future. The removal of this curse, whch has almost wrecked his life, is the greatest possible blessing that could have come to him.

P. M. D.

Now for the man's strong Christian word after five months of total abstinence, during which time the joy of the Lord has been his strength:

I am in my fifth month now, and while I am getting along nicely I am having lots of temptations, meeting them almost every minute in the day, but downing them like a good soldier. The weapon that I strike them with is suggestion, soliloquizing like this, ''Whisky is poison, and death to me, and misery to both of us. I hate it and will never touch another drop under any circumstances. Christ has delivered me from its bondage of habit, and I am a free man in Him. Sin hath no more dominion over me. I am strong in the Lord and the power of His might, saying 'no' to every temptation. He makes me strong physically, mentally, spiritually. I pray Him to make me stronger and truer every day. I thank the dear Lord with all my heart for healing my diseases and redeeming my life from destruction, and crowning me with loving kindness and tender mercies. Having reenforced myself in this fashion, you can see how able I am to knock down the next devil that I meet.''

J. H. K.

So it depends upon what the purpose of the Church may be. To the Church that regards itself a light set to shine in the darkness, the Emmanuel movement is a messenger to carry that light into all the gloomy corners of existence, that men may see the truth. To the Church that regards itself as salt that hath not lost its savor, it reveals vast human tracts that are to be kept from spoiling. To the Church that has a Christ-inspired missionary zeal it brings the despondent, the despairing, the sick, to its doors for healing, and helps the Church pour in the oil of gladness and bind up their wounds.

Such is surely enlarging the purpose of the Church.

And, oh, the need of such ministry as that! Hear Dr. Jefferson, of the Broadway Tabernacle, exclaim: "While the Church has been filled with doubts and fears, there has been an ever-deepening estrangement between the Church and large classes of our population. It is a world-wide phenomenon." And hear Dr. Parkhurst, of the Madison Square Presbyterian Church, exclaim, "It is undoubtedly the fact that there is misunderstanding between the Church and the rank and file of the working classes. The Church in times past has been excessively addicted to the work of preparing people to live in heaven, instead of fitting them to be comfortable, decent and righteous citizens of the world that now is. The step that is obligatory upon the Church is to enter more appreciatively and sympathetically into the material, intellectual and spiritual necessities of the people in this present life. We can depend upon it that people will love the Church as much as the Church loves the people. The solution of the present problem

is one which involves a more thorough forgetfulness of our own spiritual perquisites,
and a holy ambition to reproduce in ourselves
the mind with which Christ cherished all the
interests of all people.''

The Emmanuel movement would go far
to bridge Dr. Jefferson's ever-deepening
estrangement between the Church and the
people at large. It would, as no other
adaptation of the Gospel ever has, help
achieve Dr. Parkhurst's desire that the
Church make men comfortable, decent, righteous citizens of the world that now is.

Saying all this is not to affirm for an
instant that the Church should change front
upon the religious problem. It is not to
cease its endeavors to save the soul. Rather
to increase them, the body being a very tem-
porary concern in comparison. It is not to
replace its vision of the delectable hills with
that of an earth full of human wo. It is
simply called upon to consider extension, as
well as altitude, that all down along the shining line connecting the highest point of altitude with the farthest point of base petitions
for help, health and life may ascend, and down

which the angels of peace and joy and all heavenly ministration may come to bless the earth. In short, it is to realize that the field is the world; the place, the only place, where Our Lord gave us any authority to scatter the good seed of His word.

QUESTIONS AND ANSWERS

I

Please state briefly the principles of the Emmanuel
movement; also state how they can be self-applied?

The most important step forward that has occurred in psychology since I have been a student of that science is the discovery that, in certain subjects at least, there is not only the consciousness of the ordinary field with its usual center and margin, but an addition thereto in the shape of a set of memories, thoughts and feelings which are extra marginal and outside the primary consciousness altogether, yet able to reveal their presence by unmistakable signs. I call this the most important step forward, because unlike the other advances which psychology has made, this discovery has revealed to us an entirely unsuspected peculiarity in the constitution of human nature.

—William James.

I

Please state briefly the principles of the Emmanuel movement; also state how they can be self-applied?

A.—The Emmanuel movement has two sides, a psychologic and a religious. It probably would never have been born but for the revelations of modern psychology upon the existence of two minds in every person, a conscious and a subconscious. It is based on the knowledge that in the subconscious mind, or life, there are deep and far-reaching remedial powers that exert themselves instinctively along the line of the suggestion imparted to it by yourself or another person who would help you. Much is made of a quiescent relaxed state; for the suggestion you give yourself. Else what is given you by another depends upon the inactive, unquestioning, unreasoning condition of the conscious mind. During sleep these health thoughts take root in the subconscious life more quickly than at other times. If it is self-suggestion you indulge in, just before going to sleep, else when you are quiet and relaxed, is the best time. The health thought, which is really a mental picture you form, is taken eagerly by the subconscious life. It is simply an impression you make upon it. It is a hint you give, that you want worked out. You may not realize the result you desire for a long time.

But do not think the impression has not been made because you do not realize it.

The realization will come to you later, perhaps weeks after, but the more faith you have that it will come the quicker it will come, for faith is the atmosphere the subconscious mind must have, that the suggestion grow and be realized; just as the seed planted in the ground must have air and sunlight and rain to grow in else it will never spring up from the depths of the soil. If you doubt that the subconscious will grow the suggestion, you negative the suggestion and make it useless. There is great danger of doing this just because you are impatient and over anxious to realize results. Remember that the religious name for the subconscious life or mind is the soul, altho the psychologist will not concede the claim. Hudson, however, speaks of a central intelligence within us which controls bodily functions, actuates the involuntary muscles and keeps the bodily machinery in motion. "Call this intelligence," he further states, "the principle of life, the abdominal brain, the communal soul, or the subjective mind, yet it exists, and controls the body functions in health and disease." Hudson's statement, you see, will permit this religious terminology. And I am convinced in reading Hudson's book on "The Law of Mental Medicine" that he would agree with us that you can draw on the Universal Mind, which is another name for God, for the power needed to grow the health thought implanted in the soul.

Here is where we come on to religious ground. Christ is the source of the abundant life. As God's representative to man He gives this God life to whosoever takes it of Him. You can treat yourself psychologically then, or religiously. Call upon God in prayer for His life to be manifested in you to cure your ills, and believe it is given the moment you sincerely ask. This faith becomes the favorable atmosphere for it to grow and manifest itself in. To look at the question psychologically benefits you because tho you do not consciously call on God you are all the while assuming His life-giving power, for you are simply taking advantage of the divine laws put in your keeping and which psychology has revealed. Suggestion and belief in the latent power of the subconscious are divinely provided means for you to use.

II

How is it that the subconscious mind has so much
curative power?

There is a great deal of unmapped country within us.
—GEORGE ELIOT.

II

How is it that the subconscious mind has so much curative power?

A.—If, as I believe, our subconscious mind is the individual manifestation of the universal mind, it is easy to see whence comes its curative power, for no stretching of the imagination is needed to see God as the great saving force of existence. His all power can not be more wisely and lovingly used than in saving His children, in making them whole through and through and all in all.

If, on the other hand, we eliminate this conception of the subconscious mind being the individual manifestation of the universal mind, and see it to be the residential mind into which has filtered all the influences of our conscious active life, then it is to be thought of as soil potentially productive of health and good, but only after health seeds and strength thoughts have been planted

there by the normal, conscious, rational mind
either of yourself or of some one interested
in your welfare. In this case the curative
power is in the thought ideal, or health suggestion imparted. Whether the subconscious
have actual latent divine life energy, or only
potential ability to follow out your suggestion to logical remedial results, it must be
remembered that there is evil lodged there
as well as good, and destructive forces as
well as constructive. Hence the necessity
of suggestion of good to be planted in that
soil, that it sprout and spring up and choke
out the weeds of evil habit already there.

Why we speak thus hypothetically is because the subconscious is the great unin-
vestigated realm that is little more than
discovered. We do not know yet what the
quality of the gold may be, nor how much
of value it will assay to the ton. All we
know is that it is potentially full of power,
which will be actually demonstrated along
the line of the suggestion given it. Some
have asked why they do not realize their
health desire more speedily, and if it be because they lose their faith in being forced

to behold with their senses the same old diseased conditions. My answer is: Probably so. It makes a difference whether you have faith in results or not. While the important thing is to have faith enough to plant the remedial thought, the next important thing is to believe it will grow, for you are in touch with a universal scientific law. It must grow unless you negative the planted thought by planting doubt by its side. Often the more indifferent you are as to results the quicker results are realized. Anxiety, impatience induced by the presence of a diseased state are the deterrent checks to the manifestations of the subconscious good. Remove them and that subconscious good expresses itself, which it can not do while these deterrent checks are on. This can be achieved by refusing to be discouraged by the perception of the senses. Affirm to yourself that things are not always what they seem. Such stimulates faith. Of course I am speaking of functional troubles.

III

How do we get at our subconscious parts?

The thoughts that come often unsought, and as it were drop into the mind, are commonly the most valuable of any we have, and therefore should be secured because they seldom return again.

—JOHN LOCKE.

III

A.—You don't. They get at you. They
are always present just beneath the threshold
of consciousness. Remove consciousness,
toss aside reasoning, and they find you. How
hard you try to recall a name or place or
date. Think about something else, remove
attention, and the lost thing comes to you.
I thought laboriously for days over the development of a text a few weeks ago and gave
it up before going to sleep on a certain night.
Not until I gave it up, and consciously dis-
carded the text, did the sermon come. The
very morning after tossing it over it came
back, dragging a full-blown sermon in
its shining wake. You see, my subconscious
mind couldn't reveal its rich thought and development to me until I stopt thinking.
I couldn't get at it. The harder I tried,
the less I succeeded. Then when I became
still it got at me, and sent with lightning
rapidity its good things into my conscious

mind. This does not mean that thinking is useless, nor that preparation is futile. These are, on the other hand, necessary, as they are the giving of rational and strong auto-suggestion to the depths below.

But after all is done, those depths must be given their chance and allowed to express themselves, when they give back enriched and realized the truths you hopefully expected of them. You lay by little by little pennies, and silver bits, and an occasional bank-note in the savings-bank. It all lies there apparently at rest. But, no; it is working while you sleep, and accumulating at even compound interest, and some time afterward surprizes you with the consciousness of how well off you are. The subconscious mind is a veritable savings institution of the most improved kind. It always repays you with compound interest. Just keep storing away all that you find to be worth while against a rainy day. When the day of need arrives all the clouds will be rainbowed, and the darkness will be illumined as the stars shine out realizations of strength, health and good cheer.

IV

Is it the human or the divine mind that cures?

Thou great first cause, least understood.

—POPE.

God enters by a private door into each individual.

—EMERSON.

IV

Is it the human or the divine mind that cures?

A.—The divine is our first answer, because there is more of divine than of human potentiality in the subconscious. But if the curative energy comes from the suggestion offered, my second answer would be that it is the human mind that cures—as the suggestion emanates from the strong, rational, conscious mind. But the question arises, what is the nature of this remedial thought propulsion that travels so speedily to its destination. Thus the third answer is, it is the divine.

We do not dare give dogmatic answer here, because we are handling tools and conditions the nature of which we are quite ignorant. Hudson says that mental healing is in no sense a religion. Both Hudson and Schofield claim there is nothing supernatural about it. But both of these authorities rely on the reenforcements of religion. Hudson states, "Mental healing is not a religion, but true religion is a powerful auxiliary to mental healing. All experience shows that it is." Again he exclaims, "It is impossible for any right-minded person to reflect upon the law of mental healing, its universality, its adaptability to all grades of human intelligence, together with its implications of divine love, mercy and benevolence, without a feeling of profoundest reverence for the Being whose wisdom and fatherhood is thus unmistakably manifested." But when it comes to defining the nature of thought, of remedial suggestion of the mind of man, it becomes a foregone conclusion that the divine life is inextricably woven into the human and natural.

You see, the mind force that is driven on its way to the near-by or the distant person is a tremendous dynamic force. Walls do not impede it; distance does not exhaust it. It is superior to time and space. It is divine, manifesting itself in and through a so-called human mind. It is hard to define it. Science has not yet named it. It is mysterious. It works miraculously. I guess we had better say it is of God.

V

Are not you too presumptuous in demanding health of God?

In this world a man must either be anvil or hammer.
—LONGFELLOW.

V

**Are not you too presumptuous in demanding health
of God?**

A.—A man argued with me an hour one
day to convince me that it were well to ask
of God, and to believe that even beseeching
of God would be rewarded; but to demand
of Him was going too far. But there are
more failures in asking not enough than in
demanding all. If you are not sure it is His
will for you to enjoy health of soul and body,
it is becoming to tread softly in His presence
until you know His will. But if you are sure
His will spells health for every one of His
children until His children's work be done,
He will be more honored and pleased
through your demands upon Him than your
qualification of the request until it lose
its inherent force and attains not the thing
you need. Let Him qualify the demand.
You make it. He will then see your earnest-
ness and honor you for demanding your

rights. If you are conscious of being a child of God, and that you have a share in His inheritance of health and joy, demanding your share will be more likely to bring you realization than if you are too considerate to make the demand. Better to demand too much than never to demand at all. His will will regulate the supply.

But fear not the supply will be withheld because you demand its possession. Our politeness in the Father's presence often spells diffidence and lack of sterling faith. Our determination, on the other hand, to receive at His hand, that will not take no for an answer, honors Him who is more anxious to give good gifts than is earthly parent. Let not the fear of presumption hold you back.

VI

Why should the Emmanuel movement limit God in treating only functional diseases when New Thought and Christian Science do not?

There is more faith in honest doubt,
Believe me, than in half the creeds.
—TENNYSON.

VI

Why should the Emmanuel movement limit God in treating only functional diseases when New Thought and Christian Science do not?

A.—Well, the superficial answer would be because they do not and we do not want to be like them. We do not desire to be the laughing-stock of Tom, Dick and Harry, nor the ridicule of wiser men. We are not ready to reverse the most rational, most cultured, most scientific conclusions of the ages and be known far and wide by our vagaries rather than by our sanity. We believe that the powers that be are ordained of God. We believe that His blessing rests on medical and surgical skill as truly as it does upon any form of faith cure whatsoever, and perhaps a bit more so, especially if the Faith Curist attempts the impossible. Reason is as truly a divine creation as is faith.

It is given us to regulate ourselves by, lest superstition and credulity come in and usurp the throne. Moreover, God is friendly to mental processes, educational procedures, scientific investigation and conclusion. Physicians make mistakes, at times, many times and many mistakes. But they achieve vastly more good than harm, and save vastly more cases than they lose. It has not yet been scientifically demonstrated that faith saves more. Faith has safe haven for its failures—the will of God. When it loses its patient it exclaims with utmost complacency, "Oh, well, it wasn't God's will, you know, that he should recover." It is never self-condemning, never abashed, never made introspective and humiliated by its failures. If it were, it wouldn't be faith. It just wriggles out of all responsibility and cries hallelujah! It wasn't God's will, you know.

Medical science is less optimistic and more condemnatory of itself. It feels responsibility, and studies to do better next time. Call that studying groping in the dark if you like. All studying, thinking, investigating, is that. It is important, nevertheless, and its spirit is admirable. I, for one, am not yet willing to see medicine and surgery thrown into ill repute—physicians and surgeons made ash-men and street-cleaners, medical colleges destroyed, universities for the training of mental faculty closed up. We need more intellectual specialization than less, greater medical skill, keener, more laborious scientific research. Such application honors God. He is the God of the natural, as of the spiritual. He can be reverenced through the mind's reason as truly as through the heart's faith.

All this talk about limiting God is foolishness. To those speaking thus, God, methinks, is as a puffed-up giant, so conscious of His ability that when a mortal does not give Him a chance to express all His ability every time He acts, becomes resentful and grieved. For do you not see we have limited God?

Such advocates of an insulted Deity fail to see that He is always limiting Himself. Every form of nature limits Him. Were I asked to give an unbiased opinion, I would say He is more pleased when we limit Him than when we do not, for such, at least, shows we respect our own limitations, and hesitate to rush in where angels fear to tread.

VII

Why distinguish between functional and organic diseases when the Bible does not?

And so the Word had breath and wrought
With human hands the creed of creeds
In loveliness of perfect deeds,
More strong than all poetic thought.
—TENNYSON.

VII

A.—That the Bible does not is no reason we should not. Much is contained in the Bible not binding on us. Then much we have improved on. Its Mosaic institutionalism, its communistic form of society, have been bettered; its simple-life way of doing things improved. Jesus rode into Jerusalem on an ass. Two years ago I rode into Jerusalem in an easy-going vestibuled train. I think my way an improvement over His, at least for comfort. Mary and Martha lived in a sod house. You wouldn't exchange your sanitary stone dwelling, with plumbing and bath tub, just to be Scriptural, would you?

Common sense, to say nothing of reason, is needed in appreciating both the Scriptures and your own limits of efficiency. Because Christ drew no line between functional and organic maladies is no reason I should not. I compliment Him more in drawing the line than in wandering all over the field. That drawing of the line shows I consider Him a bigger man than am I. He was perfect. I am quite imperfect. He was sinless. I'm a bit otherwise at times. He had all power. I've so little that I make no boasts; in fact, am sometimes ashamed to look the little I have in the face. I am so delighted to be privileged to remedy a few functional troubles that I am heartily glad to seek medical aid for organic ones. The functionals I have attacked are so hard that I desire, up to date, to undertake nothing more difficult. It may be as easy for God to cure organic diseases as functional. But I am so rejoiced that He will condescend to be a worker with me along those functional lines that spell out about three-quarters of it all that I, Alexander-like, cry not for larger worlds to conquer.

VIII

State wherein the Emmanuel movement is an advance
on Faith Cure, Christian Science and New Thought
principles?

Be thou but self-possessed, thou hast the art of living.
—GOETHE.

VIII

State wherein the Emmanuel movement is an advance on Faith Cure, Christian Science and New Thought principles?

A.—The answer is that it is more rational, as seen in limiting the field of operation to functional diseases, and in using scientific terms and in recognizing the physician's skill as a legitimate God-given force. This rational characteristic is also seen in the keeping of records of ailments and remedial work, also where no remedy results. These records are of immense help for future reference when a physician or a psychologist wishes to know just wherein and how far these rational and religious treatments work remedially.

It should be conceded, however, that the disciples of Faith Cure, New Thought and Christian Science consider the Emmanuel movement a retrogression, inasmuch as it limits its field of operation to functional diseases. Viewpoint is everything here as elsewhere. All depends upon the degree of Omnipotence you attribute to the universal mind. To limit Omnipotent power to the functional side of life would seem to be robbing it of its distinguishing characteristic, to the making of the all-powerful only partially powerful. But a considerable measure of consistency should be ascribed to God as truly as to man. Self-limitation is not necessarily a manifestation of weakness. We do not expect God to put miraculously either human or angelic characteristics into the beasts of the jungle; nor a rational mind into the imbecile; nor new fresh vegetable life energy into the decayed tree. How deep and far-reaching a diseased condition in the human body can be divinely restored to health may be for long an open question, with intelligent advocates on either side of the tremendous issue. Moreover, the coming years of intelligence, faith and human experimentation will, it is to be hoped, remedy much of our conclusion as to what constitutes curative and non-curative malady. That all advocates of psychotherapeutics have gotten hold of, tho at different points, the same universal health principle is more to rejoice in than that their different methods of application are to be deplored. Future revelations along this line may make for further divergence or greater unity. At present it is a toss-up which. Emerson's dictum, that "Each new step we take in thought reconciles twenty seemingly discordant facts as expressions of one law," points toward greater unity.

IX

Hasn't the greatest development of character depended
on suffering? Therefore, do you not weaken character by relieving suffering?

Every man has at times in his mind the ideal of what he should be, but is not. This ideal may be high and complete or it may be quite low and insufficient; yet in all men that really seek to improve it is better than the actual character.
—THEODORE PARKER.

IX

Hasn't the greatest development of character depended on suffering? Therefore, do you not weaken character by relieving suffering?

A.—That's a good question, and intricate. Yes, character is deepened by suffering. But that it can only be deepened by suffering is not true. While he who never endures nor suffers grows up shallow and unsympathetic, too much endurance, too constant suffering may make us selfish and rebellious. There's an underlying something to be reckoned with —namely, motive—before you can say just how suffering will affect you. Every hospital and infirmary and public home of a sanatorium nature exist because some one has suffered and wants to remedy other people's suffering. But there's something better than the character that is built up through suffering; namely, that life whose suffering has been enough relieved to make him strong enough to be a minister of health to others.

Just because suffering is a good thing to develop character supposing a Christian motive to be resident there, is no reason it should not be banished, so far as possible. Why engage a doctor when ill? Why build hospital or sanatorium? Why seek redemption from any ill? Because the alleviation of suffering for character's sake and many other reasons is better than the suffering itself. Tho a sick person may develop nobility of soul, you can't tell how much nobler that character would be were the ill removed. Joy, faith, assurance of God's near remedial power, and positive regaining of health, are finer developers of character than suffering.

Then, again, all the character development dependent on suffering does not mean the presence of physical pain. Be sure there will be suffering enough left. Mental suffering, moral suffering, through sympathy, non-appreciation, positive human opposition, are all left. Jesus was called the Man of Sorrows, but it was not sorrow resulting from ill health. Christ's work in relieving suffering and disease is good precedent for us to do all we can to make sick people well.

X

What do you think of the Emmanuel movement after
four months of it? Does it pay?

The God of grace and mercy gives to each that which he craves. If we think that all is well with us He will leave us to try whether all is well. If we find that there is something that is not well, something that must be set right in us, He will set it right.

—FREDERICK DENISON MAURICE.

X

What do you think of the Emmanuel movement after four months of it? Does it pay?

A.—This question is asked by a clergyman. In answer I would say: I think it is a pretty good thing and ought to be introduced into all the churches. I think much more of it than I did at first. It has been a growing appreciation. I think it has come to stay. I think it puts a rich and beautiful content into religion and denominationalism, for it means becoming practical and helpful in a larger and more individual sense than was before possible. It also puts knowledge into a minister's mind and joy into his heart. It gives him a liberal education and a very practical one. It enables him to know men and women as he never otherwise could. It makes him sympathetic and helpful in very definite ways. It makes him more appreciated by not only those he helps, but by all truly Christian people.

Does it pay? I presume the questioner means, does it pay the church practising it. Oh, yes. It may not bring individual members into the Church. It has not done so here. But it can not help enriching the Church, just as all Christian work and missionary effort enriches it. The highest motive is not to increase a church-membership. Most all of my patients already belong to other churches, and it would be selfish to ask them to break with former ecclesiastical ties to join my church. When we send missionary money and prayer and effort into China and Africa and the Southwest, even into our own city, we do not think of numerically adding to our church-membership. We do it to Christianize them where they are. So the Emmanuel movement is not like Christian Science, demanding you must become a member of the denomination that helps you. It makes you the end of the effort, not itself the end. It is simply doing Christ's work of relieving ills and suffering, and asks no recompense for itself. But the recompense comes in many an unforeseen way.

ADVERTISEMENTS

PUBLICATIONS OF
FUNK & WAGNALLS COMPANY

NEW-THOUGHT BOOKS

HOW TO ATTAIN AND MAINTAIN PERFECT HEALTH

PRACTICAL HELP FOR ALL NERVE-SUFFERERS

Nerves in Order

The Latest Contribution to Preventive Medicine, Companion Volume to the Author's Book, "Nerves in Disorder."

By A. T. SCHOFIELD, M.D., M.R.C.S.E.

A BOOK of incalculable importance and helpfulness to every man and woman, giving, in popular form, the very latest scientific knowledge on the entire realm of physical and mental health. If your health is out of order either slightly or seriously, this book will show you how to put it straight again; or, better still, if you are in perfect health and wish your life machinery to run smoothly to a happy old age, this book will show you how it can be done.

SOME VITAL TOPICS DISCUST

Muscles and Exercise	The Nerves in Order
Health and Ill-Health	The Whole Man in Order
The Mind in Order	Eyes, Ears, Voice, Throat
The Food We Eat	The Heart in Order
The Finance of Hygiene	The Lungs in Order

"Dr. Schofield gives a great deal of sound, lucid, and practical advice on the maintenance of health in the widest sense."—*The Times*, London.

"The best way to work, the best way to play, the best way to eat, the best way to sleep—these and other matters are discust in a thoroughly plain and helpful manner. The significant feature of the book is that it is written by a man with an open outlook upon life, and not by an advocate of a theory or an ism."—*Globe-Democrat*, St. Louis.

On the subject of hygiene, digestion, exercise, and the ordering of the mind, this is one of the sanest books imaginable. We have felt considerably happier since reading it, and we wish the same comfort to others."—*Morning Post*, London.

"It is a practical handbook for believers in 'the ounce of prevention.'"—*World*, New York.

12mo, Cloth, 305 Pages. $1.50, Postpaid

Lightning Source UK Ltd.
Milton Keynes UK
UKHW020635020620
364265UK00011B/3340